TESTED BY *fire*

TRIAD COMMUNITY KITCHEN

TESTED BY *fire*
Triad Community Kitchen

Changing Lives One Recipe at a Time

Copyright © 2011 by
Second Harvest Food Bank of Northwest North Carolina (NWNC)
3655 Reed Street
Winston-Salem, North Carolina 27107

Cover Photography © by Kevin Collins
Cover Design by Gary Settle
Additional Photography © by Second Harvest Food Bank of NWNC

Paula Deen Signature Logo, page 9: Used with permission of Paula Deen Enterprises, LLC.
PAULA DEEN and the Paula Deen Signature Logo are trademarks of Paula Deen Enterprises, LLC.

This cookbook is a collection of favorite recipes, which are not necessarily original recipes.

All rights reserved. No part of this publication may be reproduced in any form or by any means, electronic or mechanical, including photocopying and recording, or by any information storage or retrieval system, without prior written permission from Second Harvest Food Bank of Northwest North Carolina.

ISBN: 978-0-615-40397-7

Published by
CommunityClassics®

An imprint of
FRP,INC
a wholly owned subsidiary of Southwestern
P.O. Box 305142
Nashville, Tennessee 37230
1-800-358-0560

Manufactured in the United States of America
First Printing: 2011
5,000 copies

This book is dedicated to
everyone in NWNC who will go to bed hungry tonight or
wake up tomorrow desperate from lack of a job.

*Thanks be to God
through Whom all things
are possible.*

This book is underwritten
in part by our good friends at
T.W. Garner Foods,
makers of

Contributors

Cookbook Steering Committee
   Deborah B. Lane—TCK administration and cookbook editor
   Karen Chandler, Marcia Cole, Erin Foster, Rachael Smith, Debbie Clark

Triad Community Kitchen Culinary Team
   Jeff Bacon, CEC CCA AAC—Director and Executive Chef
   Pam Browning—TCK Production Chef
   William Webster—TCK Banquet Chef and Alum
   Theme Adams—TCK Production Cook and Alum

   Clyde Fitzgerald—Executive Director, Second Harvest Food Bank of NWNC and introduction author

   Paula Deen—Friend to Food Banks everywhere and foreword author

Acknowledgments

As Clyde says, "always give credit to those who help you out." We want to express our gratitude to those who have assisted and inspired us on our journey.

   The late Reg Garner—Former CEO of T.W. Garner Foods (Texas Pete), former Second Harvest Food Bank of NWNC Board Chair, and good friend of the Food Bank.

American Culinary Federation
Community Culinary School of
   Charlotte
DC Central Kitchen
Downtown Restaurant Roundtable
Downtown Winston-Salem Partnership
Feeding America
Forsyth County Restaurant Association
Forsyth Technical Community College
Goodwill Industries of NWNC
Interfaith Food Shuttle, Raleigh, NC

   All of the restaurant, hotel, health care, and other food service partners who provide internship and employment opportunities for our students.

   Bishop Paul Francis Lanier—who encourages us to believe in our dreams.

The greatest good you can do for another
is not just to share your riches
but to reveal to them their own.

Benjamin Disraeli

TCK Staff (*l–r*): Theme Adams, Pam Browning, Jeff Bacon, Deborah B. Lane, William Webster

Contents

Clyde's Recipe for Success	8
Foreword by Paula Deen	9
Preface by Jeff Bacon	10

Full Bowls — 11
Empty Bowls — 12

Nibbles, Bites, and Salads — 25
Student Profile—Theme Adams — 26
Student Profile—Monique Darden — 40
Student Profile—Ed Williams — 48

Tricks of the Trade — 53

Casual Comfort — 67
Student Profile—Lester Davis — 68

Big Night Out — 85
Student Profile—Vanessa Lanier — 86
Student Profile—Otto Steele — 106

Sweets — 117
Student Profile—Jerome Timberlake — 118

Donors and Contributors	138
Index	139
Order Information	144

Clyde's Recipe for Success

Our Triad Community Kitchen students have turned past failures into success. Success is a matter of character, and each of our students has demonstrated their true character by overcoming personal problems and turning their life around. All meaningful achievements are the result of passion and perseverance, and our students demonstrate these traits every day.

Our students are real winners, but in order to win, they had to plan to win and prepare to win. This takes a real recipe, a plan to follow, that will lead to a successful and fulfilling life. At the Triad Community Kitchen, we give our students all the ingredients they need to prepare the best life for themselves and their loved ones.

Ingredients for successful life:

Never feel guilty about getting out of a bad situation.

Don't work for someone you wouldn't be proud to introduce to your mother.

If you invite trouble into your life, don't be surprised if it decides to stay.

Don't make promises you can't keep.

When you're not living up to *your* ethical standards, increase your efforts; *never* lower your standards.

Do *more* than is expected and do it *better* than is required.

Always give credit to those who help you.

Embrace change in your life.

Improve something *today*, even if it is your attitude.

Always save time for your family.

Foreword

In May of 2010, I was just delighted to visit Triad Community Kitchen (TCK) and Second Harvest Food Bank of Northwest North Carolina as part of the **Smithfield Foods Helping Hungry Homes** program in collaboration with Lowes Foods, a leading grocery chain in North Carolina.

As we walked back to the warehouse for speeches and the distribution of a lot of great pork products, I saw something that caught my eye—a wonderful kitchen! There, I was lucky enough to spend time with Chef Jeff Bacon, his staff, and students in the culinary training program, and I learned about how the students train to develop hands-on skills for jobs in the food industry, which is something that warms my heart.

I'm a firm believer in the old saying that if you give a man a fish you feed him for a day, but if you teach a man to fish you feed him for a lifetime. I think it is so special to see programs like TCK in action—equipping people with valuable life skills and offering them a second chance.

My husband Michael and I were served a delicious lunch prepared by Chef Jeff, his staff, and the TCK students. Y'all, it just about knocked my socks off! I was so impressed with the meal and what they are doing in their first-rate program, and this cookbook is certainly a testament to what these students can accomplish with a little bit of hard work.

You'll find some of their real-life stories in this book, plus lots of great recipes. Enjoy!

Love and best dishes,

Paula Deen

Preface

When I look back at what has happened since we began the Triad Community Kitchen in 2006, the manifest blessings are so evident. I have been given the opportunity to engage with people from all walks of life, sometimes providing them much needed help, but more often receiving and giving a gift of connection and relationship that goes far deeper than just the basic needs of life. Through the universal medium of food, I get to work with our students as they sort out the struggles of life. We walk through problems big and small together.

Issues such as low self-esteem, criminal backgrounds, substance abuse and addiction, unemployability, physical and mental limitations, and just the external factors of the economy and job shortages can all be addressed through the communication and learning that occurs in our kitchen and classroom. We strive to start people on the path to self-reliance, stressing that our program is just the beginning of the educational process. We seek to instill a passion for food, learning, and self-improvement in our students, for if they depart here thinking that they have reached some kind of conclusion to their stories they are fated to repeat past mistakes. However, if they leave us infected with a hunger to learn, grow, and cook, then we have done our job well.

All of the stories at TCK do not have happy endings, but far more do than could be achieved through human effort alone. We gladly welcome the miraculous and the supernatural at the Triad Community Kitchen. Many have likened our program to "culinary boot camp," and indeed the path to success here is hard and, at times, stressful. Our students need all of the help they can get, so a little divine intervention is always part of our strategy. We learn to rely on others, sometimes for the first time in our lives. The growth can be painful, but the rewards can be spellbinding. Our alumni have gone on to run their own culinary teams and open their own restaurants, but most to simply work, learn, and move forward in a progressive and satisfying way. They can take pride in knowing that once they graduate from TCK they have truly been, "Tested by Fire."

Jeff Bacon, CEC CCA AAC
Founding Director and Executive Chef
Triad Community Kitchen

Full Bowls

Triad Community Kitchen

Empty Bowls

Empty Bowls **is Second Harvest Food Bank of Northwest NC's Annual Signature event presented by Texas Pete Sauces.** Held each year in April on Administrative Professionals' Day, this awareness and fund-raising event is one of the most anticipated events of the season in Winston-Salem, offering great food prepared and donated by area restaurants, live music, and a fabulous silent auction.

For a donation of **$25 in advance or $30 at the door**, guests enjoy a savory soup lunch, complete with salad, fresh bread, dessert, and a drink, and they get to choose a handcrafted pottery bowl designed and donated by area artists to take home. Soup selections are not served in the bowls. Rather, they remain empty during the event as a reminder of those in need who face "empty bowls" every day.

Proceeds benefit our food distribution program, which operates to transport, collect, inspect, sort, and distribute donated food to more than 400 nonprofit organizations dedicated to feeding people at risk of hunger and others in need.

Proceeds also benefit our Kids Café program, which aims to address childhood hunger by providing youth at risk of hunger with an evening meal, tutoring, and enrichment activities three nights a week throughout the year in a safe and nurturing environment. We currently operate 10 Kids Cafés serving 500-plus youth annually.

This chapter contains recipes from many of our restaurant partners who have donated their soup creations to the event as well as some of our own specialties. We have named the chapter "Full Bowls" to reflect our efforts to fill the "Empty Bowls" that are targeted by this event.

Bayou Bean Soup

2 1/4 cups dried pinto beans
1 cup finely diced onion
2 tablespoons chicken
  bouillon granules
1 tablespoon minced garlic
1 tablespoon pepper
Ham bones (optional)
1 cup finely diced bell pepper

1/4 cup finely diced chile peppers
1/4 cup vegetable oil or margarine
1 1/2 pounds ham, diced
2 cups tomato purée
2 cups ketchup
1 tablespoon Cajun seasoning
1 tablespoon Texas Pete Hot Sauce®

Rinse and pick the beans. Combine with water to cover in a large bowl. Let stand overnight. Drain the beans and combine with 8 cups water, the onion, chicken bouillon, garlic and pepper in a large stockpot. Add the ham bones and bring to a boil. Simmer for 1 hour or until the beans are just cooked through but still firm. Remove the ham bones.

Sweat the bell pepper and chile peppers in the oil in a saucepan until tender. Add to the soup. Stir in the remaining ingredients. Simmer for 20 to 40 minutes or until the soup is the desired consistency. *Serves 12*

Navy Bean and Ham Soup

1 cup dried navy beans
2 tablespoons chicken bouillon
  granules
Salt to taste
1 cup diced celery

1/2 cup diced carrots
1/2 cup diced onion
1 pound ham, diced
2 tablespoons margarine
Pepper to taste

Rinse and pick the beans. Combine with water to cover in a large bowl. Let stand overnight. Drain the beans and combine with 8 cups water, the chicken bouillon and salt in a large stockpot. Cook for 45 to 60 minutes or until tender.

Sweat the celery, carrots, onion and ham in the margarine in a saucepan until tender. Add to the beans and season with salt and pepper. Simmer for 20 minutes or until the beans begin to break down and thicken the soup slightly. *Serves 12*

Pasta e Fagioli

1 1/4 cups dried pinto beans
8 cups water
1 meaty smoked ham hock
1/4 cup chicken base or chicken bouillon granules
1/2 cup finely diced frozen bacon
1/2 cup diced onion
1/2 cup diced celery
1/2 cup diced carrots
2 teaspoons minced garlic
2 cups canned diced tomatoes
1/4 tablespoon oregano
1 cup uncooked small pasta shells
Grated Parmigiano cheese, for garnish

Rinse and pick the beans. Combine with enough water to cover in a large bowl. Let stand overnight.

Drain the beans and combine with 8 cups water, the ham hock and chicken base in a large stockpot. Bring to a simmer and cook for 2 hours or until tender.

Sauté the bacon, onion, celery, carrots and garlic in a large nonstick skillet until tender. Add to the soup. Stir in the tomatoes and oregano. Simmer for 30 minutes. Remove the ham hock and cut the meat from the bone. Discard the bone and add the meat to the soup.

Cook the pasta in boiling water in a saucepan just until al dente. Drain and add to the soup. Heat to serving temperature. Serve with croutons or bread on top and garnish with grated Parmigiano or other hard Italian cheese. *Serves 12*

Cream of Broccoli Soup

6 cups chopped broccoli
3/4 cup clarified butter
3/4 cup diced onion
1/2 cup diced parsnip
1/4 cup diced celery

11 cups Classic Velouté (page 59)
1 Sachet D'Epices (page 65)
1 1/2 cups heavy cream, heated
1 tablespoon salt
3/4 teaspoon white pepper

Reserve 1/4 of the broccoli florets for garnish. Blanch the reserved florets in boiling water in a saucepan; drain and plunge into ice water to stop the cooking process. Melt the butter in a stockpot. Add the onion, parsnip, celery and broccoli stems. Sweat until the vegetables are tender, adding the remaining broccoli florets toward the end of the cooking time. Add the Classic Velouté and simmer for 35 to 45 minutes. Add the Sachet D'Epices and simmer for 15 minutes longer. Remove the Sachet and process the soup in several batches. Strain back into the stockpot through a fine mesh strainer. Return the soup to a simmer and add the cream. Season with the salt and white pepper. Heat the reserved broccoli florets to top the servings. *Serves 12*

Grandma's Country Chicken Soup

3/4 cup chopped yellow onion
1/4 cup chopped celery
1/4 cup chopped carrots
1/2 cup white wine
1/2 chicken, deboned and chopped

1/4 cup Italian seasoning
2 tablespoons minced garlic
4 cups chicken stock
Salt and pepper to taste
1 cup all-purpose flour

Sauté the onion, celery and carrots in a nonstick saucepan over medium heat until tender. Stir in the wine and cook until the wine has nearly evaporated. Add the chicken and sauté until partially cooked. Stir in the Italian seasoning and garlic. Sauté for 5 minutes longer. Stir in the stock and season with salt and pepper. Bring to a simmer. Sift in the flour and cook until thickened, stirring constantly. *Serves 8*

6th & Vine Restaurant, Winston-Salem, NC

Chicken Noodle Soup TCK

9 cups chicken broth
1/4 cup chicken bouillon granules
3/4 cup chopped onion
1/2 cup chopped carrots
1/2 cup chopped celery

1 tablespoon vegetable oil
2 cups chopped cooked chicken
2 tablespoons chopped parsley
Salt and white pepper to taste
1 cup uncooked egg noodles

Bring the broth and chicken bouillon to a boil in a saucepan. Sauté the onion, carrots and celery lightly in the oil in a nonstick skillet. Add to the simmering broth and simmer for 30 minutes or until the vegetables are tender. Stir in the chicken, parsley, salt and white pepper. Simmer for 10 minutes. Add the noodles and simmer for 10 minutes longer or just until the noodles are tender. For extra flavor, you can substitute Basic Chicken Stock (page 63) for the broth and bouillon. *Serves 12*

Chicken Tortilla Soup

4 cups chopped yellow onions
4 cups chopped carrots
4 cups chopped celery
4 cups chopped red bell peppers
1/2 cup chopped garlic
1/4 cup vegetable oil
24 cups chicken stock
16 cups chopped tomatoes

1/4 cup cumin
1/4 cup chopped cilantro
2 tablespoons dried Mexican oregano
2 tablespoons kosher salt
2 cups crushed corn tortilla chips
4 cups (16 ounces) shredded Pepper
   Jack cheese

Sauté the onions, carrots, celery, bell peppers and garlic in the oil in a large stockpot until tender. Add the stock, tomatoes, cumin, cilantro, oregano and kosher salt. Bring to a simmer and cook over medium heat for 20 minutes. Stir in the tortilla chips and simmer for 10 minutes longer. Purée the mixture with an immersion blender. Add the cheese and serve. *Serves 32*

Firebirds Wood Fired Grill

Chicken Corn Chowder

1/2 cup diced onion
1/4 cup diced celery
1/4 cup diced bacon
2 tablespoons all-purpose flour
3 cups diced potatoes
1 1/2 cups corn
4 cups milk
2 cups cream
2 cups chicken broth
1 pound chicken, cooked and diced
1 tablespoon minced garlic
1 tablespoon salt
1/2 teaspoon pepper
1/4 cup cornstarch (optional)

Sweat the onion and celery with the bacon in a stockpot until the vegetables are very tender. Add the flour and cook for 2 minutes or until thickened, stirring constantly. Add the potatoes, corn, milk, cream and broth; mix well. Bring to a simmer and cook for 30 minutes. Stir in the chicken, garlic, salt and pepper. Cook for 20 minutes longer. Adjust the seasoning. Thicken with a slurry of the cornstarch and 1/4 cup water if needed for the desired consistency. For extra flavor, you can substitute Basic Chicken Stock (page 63) for the broth. *Serves 12*

Clam Chowder

1/2 cup (1 stick) unsalted butter
1/2 cup crumbled cooked bacon
3/4 cup finely diced celery
1/2 cup finely diced yellow onion
1/2 cup (or less) all-purpose flour
2 cups diced undrained canned clams
1 1/2 cups clam juice
1 cup diced undrained canned potatoes
1 tablespoon kosher salt
1/2 teaspoon white pepper
2 cups heavy cream

Melt the butter in a heavy stockpot over medium heat. Add the bacon, celery and onion. Sauté until the vegetables are translucent and tender. Stir in the flour and cook for 10 minutes or until the roux is pale yellow and has a nutty aroma, stirring constantly.

Stir in the clams and clam juice. Simmer for 20 minutes. Add the potatoes and simmer for 15 minutes or until thickened to the desired consistency. Season with kosher salt and white pepper. Stir in the cream and simmer for 15 minutes, stirring frequently. Adjust the seasonings and serve hot. *Serves 4 to 6*

Village Tavern Restaurant, Winston-Salem, NC

Sweet Corn Chowder

1 1/2 cups chopped bacon
1 cup finely diced onion
1 cup finely diced celery
1/2 cup (or less) all-purpose flour
8 cups chicken stock

2 cups finely diced potatoes
4 cups corn
1 cup milk
1 cup heavy cream
Salt and pepper to taste

Render the bacon in a large stockpot. Drain off excess drippings, reserving enough to sweat the vegetables. Add the onion and celery to the drippings and sweat until translucent. Stir in the flour and cook to form a blonde roux, stirring constantly. Add the stock in batches, stirring constantly until smooth after each addition. Simmer for 30 minutes. Add the potatoes and simmer for 10 minutes. Stir in the corn. Simmer until the corn and potatoes are cooked through. Stir in the milk and cream; season with salt and pepper. *Serves 16*

River Birch Lodge, Winston-Salem, NC

Roasted Red Pepper Seafood Chowder

4 carrots, diced
4 ribs celery, diced
1 large white onion, diced
6 potatoes, peeled and diced
3 tablespoons minced garlic
3 tablespoons Old Bay seasoning
6 1/2 cups canned crushed tomatoes
4 cups heavy cream

3 cups puréed roasted red peppers
2 cups clam juice
4 ounces tilapia, diced
4 ounces salmon, diced
4 ounces mahimahi, diced
Salt and pepper to taste
1 1/2 cups sherry
Cornstarch (optional)

Sweat the carrots, celery and onion in a large nonstick stockpot until tender. Add the potatoes, garlic and Old Bay seasoning; sweat for 2 to 3 minutes longer. Stir in the tomatoes, cream, roasted peppers and clam juice. Bring to a simmer and cook until the potatoes are tender. Add the tilapia, salmon and mahimahi. Simmer for 5 minutes over low heat. Season with salt and pepper and finish with the sherry. Thicken with a slurry of equal parts cornstarch and water if needed for the desired consistency. *Serves 24*

NOMA Restaurant and Wine Bar, Winston-Salem, NC

Minestrone

1 cup dried pinto beans
10 cups water
1/4 cup vegetable bouillon granules
1/2 cup diced red bell pepper
1/2 cup diced green bell pepper
1 cup diced onion
1 cup diced carrots
1 cup diced celery

1 tablespoon minced garlic
2 tablespoons Italian seasoning
1 cup uncooked pasta shells
1 cup small cauliflower florets
1 cup (1/4-inch) zucchini slices
1 cup (1/4-inch) summer
   squash slices
Salt and pepper to taste

Rinse and pick the beans. Combine with enough water to cover in a bowl and let stand overnight.

Drain the beans and combine with 10 cups water and the vegetable bouillon in a large stockpot. Bring to a simmer.

Sweat the bell peppers, onion, carrots, celery and garlic in a nonstick skillet until tender. Add to the soup with the Italian seasoning. Stir in the pasta and cauliflower. Cook for 8 minutes. Add the zucchini and summer squash and cook for 3 minutes longer. Season with salt and pepper. You can substitute canned beans for the dried beans. *Serves 16*

Lentil Soup

1 cup dried black lentils
8 cups water
2 cups Swiss chard
1/4 cup vegetable oil
1/2 cup diced onion

1 tablespoon minced garlic
1/4 cup lemon juice
1 tablespoon olive oil
Salt to taste

Rinse and pick the lentils. Combine with the water in a saucepan and cook over medium heat just until the lentils are tender. Add the Swiss chard and cook for 10 to 15 minutes or until tender.

Heat the vegetable oil in a skillet. Add the onion and garlic and sauté until caramelized. Add to the soup and stir in the lemon juice and olive oil. Cook until the lentils are as tender as desired, adding hot water if needed for the desired consistency. Season with salt and serve hot with toasted bread. *Serves 10*

Mooney's Mediterranean Café

Chilled Gazpacho

2 1/2 cucumbers, peeled and diced
2 onions, diced
2 teaspoons minced garlic
1 1/2 cups beef consommé or
   beef broth
2 1/2 cups tomato sauce
1 (15-ounce) can diced tomatoes
2/3 cup wine vinegar
1 cup vegetable oil
2 tablespoons Worcestershire sauce
Cucumber slices, for garnish

Combine the cucumbers, onion and garlic in a large plastic container. Add the consommé, tomato sauce, tomatoes, vinegar, oil and Worcestershire sauce; mix well. Chill in the refrigerator for 2 hours or up to 3 days. Serve in chilled bowls garnished with cucumber slices. *Serves 8*

Ryan's Restaurant

Tomato Bisque

2 shallots, chopped
1 tablespoon olive oil
1 tablespoon butter
8 cups canned tomato fillets
3 cups chicken stock
1 tablespoon tomato paste
Dash of cayenne pepper
1/2 cup heavy cream
Salt and black pepper to taste
2 tablespoons chopped basil,
   for garnish

Sauté the shallots in the olive oil and butter in a saucepan. Stir in the tomatoes, stock, tomato paste and cayenne pepper. Cook until heated through. Process the soup with an immersion blender or in a food processor. Combine with the cream in the saucepan and bring to a simmer. Season with salt and black pepper. Garnish servings with the basil. *Serves 12*

Mozelle's Restaurant, Winston-Salem, NC

Creamy Tomato Basil Soup

1 1/2 tablespoons vegetable oil
3/4 onion, finely diced
1 1/2 garlic cloves, minced
3 cups chicken broth
2 cups crushed tomatoes
1 cup tomato purée

1 1/2 tablespoons sugar
1 teaspoon salt
1/2 teaspoon pepper
2 cups heavy cream
3/4 cup chopped fresh basil
Additional basil and croutons, for garnish

Heat the oil in a large heavy saucepan. Add the onion and sweat over medium heat until tender. Add the garlic and cook for 2 minutes. Stir in the broth, tomatoes and tomato purée. Season with the sugar, salt and pepper. Simmer for 5 minutes. Stir in the cream and return to a simmer. Stir in 3/4 cup basil at serving time. Garnish with additional basil and croutons. *Serves 12*

White Chicken Chili

3 cups dried navy beans
8 cups water
1/4 cup chicken bouillon granules or chicken base
1 cup diced onion
1/4 cup diced bell pepper
2 tablespoons finely diced fresh mild chiles
1 tablespoon minced garlic
1 1/2 pounds chicken, cooked, deboned and chopped

2 tablespoons diced canned jalalpeño chiles
1 tablespoon Texas Pete Hot Sauce®
1 tablespoon chili powder
1 tablespoon cumin
1 tablespoon Cajun seasoning
1 tablespoon sugar
1 tablespoon salt
1/4 teaspoon pepper
Cornstarch (optional)

Rinse and pick the beans. Combine with enough water to cover in a large bowl. Let stand overnight. Drain the beans and combine with 8 cups water and the chicken bouillon in a large stockpot. Simmer for 1 hour.

Sauté the onion, bell pepper, mild chiles and garlic in a nonstick skillet until tender. Add to the beans. Stir in the chicken, jalapeño chiles, hot sauce, chili powder, cumin, Cajun seasoning, sugar, salt and pepper. Bring to a simmer and adjust the seasonings. Thicken with a slurry of equal parts cornstarch and water if needed for the desired consistency. *Serves 12*

Black Bean and Ham Chili

2 cups dried black beans
8 cups water
1 cup diced onion
1/2 cup diced bell pepper
1 tablespoon minced jalapeño chile
1 tablespoon minced garlic
1 pound ham, diced
1 cup canned diced tomatoes
1 cup tomato purée
1/4 cup Texas Pete Hot Sauce®
2 tablespoons chicken bouillon granules
2 tablespoons cumin
1 tablespoon chili powder
1 teaspoon salt
1/2 teaspoon pepper

Rinse and pick the beans. Combine with enough water to cover in a large bowl. Let stand overnight.

Drain the beans and combine with 8 cups water and the onion in a large stockpot. Bring to a boil and cook just until tender.

Sweat the bell pepper, jalapeño chile and garlic in a nonstick skillet until tender. Add to the beans. Stir in the ham, tomatoes, tomato purée, hot sauce, chicken bouillon, cumin, chili powder, salt and pepper. Simmer for 30 to 45 minutes or until the soup is the desired consistency. Adjust the seasoning to serve. For extra flavor, you can substitute Basic Chicken Stock (page 63) for the 8 cups water and chicken bouillon. *Serves 12*

Chili Con Carne TCK

2 pounds ground beef
1 cup chopped onion
1/4 cup minced garlic
1/2 cup water
1 tablespoon beef bouillon granules
1/4 cup diced bell pepper
2 tablespoons minced jalapeño chile
1/4 cup sugar
2 tablespoons chili powder
1 tablespoon cumin
1 teaspoon salt
1 teaspoon pepper
4 cups drained canned kidney beans
4 cups tomato purée
1/4 cup Texas Pete Hot Sauce®

Brown the ground beef with the onion, garlic, water and beef bouillon in a stockpot, stirring until the ground beef is crumbly; drain. Add the bell pepper, jalapeño chile, sugar, chili powder, cumin, salt and pepper. Simmer for 10 minutes. Stir in the beans, tomato purée and hot sauce. Simmer for 10 minutes longer. Adjust the seasonings to serve. *Serves 12*

Ballymoe (Irish Stew)

2 1/2 to 3 pounds boned gigot or rack-cut
   (1-inch) lamb chops, deboned
12 pearl onions, or 4 small onions, coarsely diced
12 baby carrots, or 8 medium carrots, coarsely diced
Salt and freshly ground pepper to taste
3 1/2 cups lamb stock or other stock or broth
12 small red or white potatoes
1 sprig of thyme
1 tablespoon all-purpose flour
1 tablespoon butter, melted
1 tablespoon chopped fresh parsley
1 tablespoon chopped fresh chives

Trim and reserve the excess fat from the lamb. Cut the lamb into large chunks. Render the reserved fat in a heavy saucepan over low heat; discard the rendered pieces. Add the lamb to the hot drippings in the saucepan and sauté until light brown. Remove to a bowl, reserving the drippings in the saucepan. Sauté the onions and carrots lightly in the drippings in the saucepan. Alternate layers of the lamb and vegetables in a Dutch oven or heavy roasting pan, seasoning each layer with salt and pepper. Add the stock to the drippings in the saucepan and stir to deglaze the saucepan. Pour into the Dutch oven. Top with the potatoes and sprinkle with salt and pepper. Add the thyme.

Bring to a boil on the stovetop; cover with baking parchment and the lid. Bake at 350 degrees or simmer on the stovetop for 1 to 1 1/2 hours or until tender. Pour the cooking liquid into a saucepan and skim off any grease. Bring to a simmer. Stir the flour into the melted butter in a heavy skillet. Cook over low heat for 2 minutes, stirring occasionally. Add to the simmering cooking liquid and cook until thickened, stirring constantly. Adjust the seasoning and add the parsley and chives. Pour back into the Dutch oven. Return to a simmer to serve. *Serves 12*

Finnegan's Wake Irish Pub, Winston-Salem, NC

Nibbles, Bites, and Salads

Triad Community Kitchen

Theme Adams
Cloverdale Kitchen

There is an old saying, "Stick with the winners if you want to win." Apparently Theme Adams is a big believer in that saying.

After his graduation from the Triad Community Kitchen Culinary Training Program in July 2009, there were no jobs in Winston-Salem. The economy had bottomed out, and several restaurants were closing their doors permanently, creating a surplus of available food service workers. It was the worst time to be looking for a job.

Theme moved back in with his mother and was trying to piece together a life complicated by bad decisions. The father of seven children and a participant in a string of low-paying fast food jobs, Theme was suffocating under the burden of unpaid child support. Incarceration was a constant threat, and the future looked bleak. He could have given up, but he wanted to keep learning.

Theme showed up after graduation to volunteer at the TCK kitchen, helping out with our prepared meals program and with caterings. He put in forty hours many weeks, helping, learning, and changing his outlook. He was determined that when an opportunity came around, he would not miss it.

Eventually a call came in from Nan Griswold, the retired former Executive Director of the Second Harvest Food Bank (where TCK is housed), informing us that her friend John Cortesis of Cloverdale Kitchen was looking for a serving cook. I called and spoke with John about Theme and his exceptional willingness and determination, and then sent Theme over to speak with them about the job. He was hired, and a couple weeks later our production cook position here at TCK opened up.

We had many TCK alumni interested, but our comfort level with Theme's work ethic and the fact that he was already totally trained from all of his volunteer hours here tipped the scale in his favor. In March of 2010 he became a part of the TCK staff. Theme is a vital part of our team and autonomously handles the bulk foods cookery in our kitchen.

Theme has his financial obligations under control now. He says of his experiences at TCK, "TCK works. You have to want to learn and want to be a chef. It's life changing if you are willing to change."

Spanakopita

4 bunches scallions, chopped
3 bunches leeks, chopped
2 cups chopped fresh spinach
8 eggs, beaten
2 cups crumbled feta cheese
1 cup cottage cheese
1/2 cup vegetable oil
2 tablespoons salt
2 tablespoons pepper
1 (16-ounce) package frozen phyllo dough, thawed
1 cup (2 sticks) butter, melted

Preheat the oven to 350 degrees. Combine the scallions, leeks and spinach in a mixing bowl. Add the eggs, feta cheese, cottage cheese, oil, salt and pepper; mix well.

Reserve five sheets of the phyllo dough under a damp cloth. Layer five of the remaining sheets of phyllo dough in a 9×13-inch baking dish, folding any excess into the dish. Use a pastry brush to brush the layers with the butter. Sprinkle a light layer of the vegetable mixture over the phyllo sheets.

Alternate layers of a single sheet of phyllo dough with a sprinkling of the vegetable mixture to the top of the dish, brushing each sheet of phyllo dough with the butter. Top with the reserved five sheets of phyllo dough and brush with butter.

Cut into twelve servings, cutting halfway through the layers. Bake for 1 hour. Cut the remaining way through the layers to serve. *Serves 12*

John Cortesis and Theme Adams, Cloverdale Kitchen

Texas Pete® Buffalo Chicken Dip

8 ounces cream cheese, softened
1/2 cup blue cheese salad dressing or ranch salad dressing
1/2 cup (4 ounces) shredded mozzarella cheese, or
   1/2 cup crumbled blue cheese
1/2 cup Texas Pete Buffalo Wing Sauce®
2 cups shredded cooked chicken

Preheat the oven to 350 degrees. Beat the cream cheese in a mixing bowl until smooth. Spread evenly in a deep baking dish. Combine the blue cheese dressing, mozzarella cheese and wing sauce in a large mixing bowl and mix well. Stir in the chicken. Spoon over the cream cheese. Bake for 20 minutes or until heated through. Serve with chips or vegetables. *Serves 12 to 16*

Garner Foods

Smokin' Pimento Cheese Spread

16 ounces smoked Cheddar cheese
4 ounces roasted red peppers, diced
1 tablespoon (or more) mayonnaise
4 ounces sweet Vidalia onion relish

Grate the cheese into the bowl of a mixer fitted with a paddle attachment; beat until smooth. Add the roasted peppers, mayonnaise and onion relish; mix well, adding additional mayonnaise if needed for the desired consistency. Serve with bread or crostini. *Serves 12*

Corn and Leek Pancakes

1/2 cup yellow cornmeal
1/2 cup all-purpose flour
3/4 teaspoon baking powder
1/2 teaspoon salt
1/2 cup sweet corn

1/2 cup minced leeks
1 tablespoon chopped bell pepper
1/4 cup (1/2 stick) butter, melted
3/4 cup milk
1 egg

Mix the cornmeal, flour, baking powder and salt in a bowl.
Mince the corn in a food processor. Sauté the corn, leeks and bell pepper in the butter in a skillet until tender. Stir in the milk. Remove from the heat and add the egg; mix well. Add the dry ingredients and mix until moistened.
Spoon the batter by 1/4 cupfuls onto a griddle or large nonstick skillet. Cook until golden brown on both sides. *Serves 4*

Crab Cakes

1 pound crab claw meat
1 egg
1 cup crushed saltine crackers
1/4 cup finely diced celery
1/4 cup finely diced onion
1/4 cup vegetable oil

2 tablespoons Dijon mustard
1 tablespoon Old Bay seasoning
1 tablespoon lemon juice
1 tablespoon hot sauce
2 tablespoons vegetable oil

Combine the crab meat with the egg, cracker crumbs, celery and onion in a bowl. Add 1/4 cup oil, the Dijon mustard, Old Bay seasoning, lemon juice and hot sauce; mix well. Chill until needed.
Shape the crab mixture into ten cakes. Heat 2 tablespoons oil in a skillet over medium heat. Add the crab cakes and sauté until cooked through and brown on both sides. *Serves 10*

Cheese Grits Cakes

1 tablespoon butter
1/2 cup finely diced sweet onion
1 garlic clove, minced
1 1/2 cups uncooked white stone-ground grits
3 cups (or more) chicken stock
1 1/2 cups heavy cream
1 teaspoon coarsely ground pepper
2 cups (8 ounces) shredded sharp white Cheddar cheese
1 cup (4 ounces) grated Parmesan cheese
1/4 cup chopped scallions
1 tablespoon canola oil

Melt the butter in a saucepan. Add the onion and garlic and sweat until tender. Add the grits and mix well. Stir in the stock and simmer over low heat until the liquid is absorbed. Add the cream and pepper. Simmer over low heat for 35 to 45 minutes or until smooth and creamy, adding additional stock if needed for the desired consistency. Stir in the Cheddar cheese, Parmesan cheese and scallions.

Spread the grits evenly in a 13×18-inch pan lined with baking parchment. Chill overnight or until very firm. Cut into 1-inch rounds.

Heat the canola oil in a nonstick skillet until very hot. Add the grits cakes and sear quickly on both sides. *Serves 12*

Top this Carolina favorite with your choice of savory topping.

Seared Grits Cakes with Crisp Country Ham and Chiffonade of Collards

4 cups fresh collard greens
8 ounces country ham, sliced
1 teaspoon canola oil
Salt and pepper to taste
1/4 cup (1 ounce) grated Parmesan cheese
Cheese Grits Cakes (page 30)

Preheat the oven to 350 degrees. Wash the collard greens and trim the tough center ribs. Roll into tubes and cut crosswise into very thin strips (chiffonade).

Place the country ham on a baking sheet and bake until brown and crisp. Cool slightly.

Heat the canola oil in a nonstick saucepan and add the collard greens; season with salt and pepper. Cook just until the greens are slightly wilted and bright green, stirring frequently.

Break or cut the country ham into pieces about the same size as the Cheese Grits Cakes. Top the grits cakes with the ham, collard greens and Parmesan cheese. *Serves 12*

Chive Parmesan Crackers

1 cup (4 ounces) grated
  Parmesan cheese
3/4 cup all-purpose flour
1/2 cup (1 stick) butter, chilled
  and diced

2 tablespoons chopped chives
2 tablespoons chopped Italian parsley
1 garlic clove, minced
1 teaspoon salt
2 tablespoons balsamic vinegar

Combine the cheese, flour, butter, chives, parsley, garlic and salt in a mixer fitted with a paddle attachment. Mix at low speed until the mixture has the consistency of small peas. Add the vinegar and mix to form a soft dough. Wrap and chill in the refrigerator for 1 hour or longer.

Preheat the oven to 375 degrees. Roll the pastry on a lightly floured surface and cut as desired. Place on a baking sheet and bake for 10 to 15 minutes or until light brown. *Serves 12*

Grilled Asparagus with Prosciutto

24 asparagus spears
1 teaspoon olive oil
Salt and pepper to taste

6 slices prosciutto
1 teaspoon Balsamic Glaze
  (page 54)

Preheat the grill. Trim 2 inches from the stem ends of the asparagus spears. Toss with the olive oil and season with salt and pepper. Grill over high heat for 2 to 4 minutes or until char-marked. Cool slightly.

Cut the prosciutto slices into halves lengthwise and then into halves crosswise. Wrap each asparagus spear with a slice of prosciutto. Drizzle with the Balsamic Glaze to serve. *Serves 12*

Chicken Satay

1 cup finely diced onion
2 teaspoons minced garlic
6 tablespoons corn oil
2 1/2 cups water
1 1/3 cups peanut butter
1 tablespoon curry powder
2 teaspoons brown sugar

4 teaspoons soy sauce
2 teaspoons lemon juice
1 teaspoon chili powder
Salt and pepper to taste
2 pounds boneless skinless
  chicken breasts, cut into strips

Preheat the grill or broiler. Sauté the onion and garlic in the corn oil in a saucepan until golden brown. Stir in the water, peanut butter, curry powder and brown sugar. Simmer until thickened and smooth. Add the soy sauce, lemon juice, chili powder, salt and pepper. Skewer the chicken strips on bamboo skewers that have been soaked in water. Grill or broil until cooked through, brushing with the peanut sauce near the end of the cooking time. Serve with the remaining peanut sauce. *Serves 10*

Chicken and Sun-Dried Tomato Meatballs

1/2 cup minced onion
1 tablespoon minced garlic
1 tablespoon olive oil
1 pound ground chicken
2 eggs
3/4 cup bread crumbs

1/2 cup (2 ounces) grated Parmesan
  cheese
1/4 cup chopped oil-pack
  sun-dried tomatoes
1 tablespoon minced parsley
1 tablespoon salt
1 teaspoon pepper

Preheat the oven to 425 degrees. Sauté the onion and garlic in the olive oil in a skillet until tender; cool to room temperature. Combine with the remaining ingredients in a bowl; mix well. Shape into thirty-two tablespoon-size meatballs and arrange on a baking sheet. Bake for 15 minutes or to an internal temperature of 165 degrees. *Serves 12*

Meatballs in Chipotle Sauce

Chipotle Sauce
2 cups diced onions
4 teaspoons minced garlic
2 tablespoons vegetable oil
2 cups tomato sauce
4 ounces canned chipotle chiles in adobo sauce, mashed
1 cup beef broth

Meatballs
1 pound ground beef
1 pound ground pork or sausage
2/3 cup finely diced onion
2 eggs, beaten
1/4 cup all-purpose flour
2 tablespoons minced cilantro
1 teaspoon oregano
1/2 teaspoon cumin
3 tablespoons vegetable oil

    Sauce: Sauté the onions and garlic in the oil in a saucepan until tender. Add the tomato sauce, chipotle chiles and broth and mix well. Simmer for 15 minutes. Process the sauce in a food processor or with an immersion blender until smooth; return to the saucepan.
    Meatballs: Preheat the oven to 350 degrees. Combine the ground beef, ground pork, onion, eggs, flour, cilantro, oregano and cumin in a bowl and mix well. Shape into 1/2-inch balls. Brown in the oil in an ovenproof skillet. Bake for 15 minutes or until the meatballs register 155 degrees internally. Add to the sauce and simmer until heated through. *Serves 12*

Balsamic-Glazed Peaches with Prosciutto

1/4 cup balsamic vinegar
1/4 cup honey
6 peaches, peeled and each cut into 8 wedges
1 ounce prosciutto, sliced paper-thin and cut into strips
1 tablespoon vegetable oil

Combine the vinegar and honey in a small saucepan and bring to a simmer. Simmer until syrupy and reduced by one-half; the glaze will continue to thicken slightly as it cools.

Wrap each peach wedge with one strip of prosciutto. Sear the wedges in the oil in a skillet until the prosciutto is light brown. Drizzle with just enough balsamic glaze to coat the peaches. Serve warm or at room temperature. *Serves 12*

Teriyaki Pineapple with Brie, Bacon and Chiles

1/2 fresh pineapple
6 ounces brie cheese
3 slices bacon, partially cooked
2 tablespoons teriyaki glaze and basting sauce
1 serrano chile or datil chile, very thinly sliced

Preheat the oven to 425 to 450 degrees. Trim the pineapple and cut into twenty-four (1/4-inch-thick) slices. Cut the brie cheese and bacon into the same size pieces. Layer one slice of pineapple, one piece of bacon and one slice of brie for each canapé and top each stack with a second slice of pineapple. Arrange the stacks on a baking sheet and brush with the teriyaki glaze and basting sauce. Bake just until the cheese begins to melt and the stacks begin to brown. Top each with a slice or two of the sliced chile and serve warm. *Serves 12*

Pulled Pork Crostini

12 slices French baguette
1 tablespoon olive oil
Salt and pepper to taste
4 ounces farmer's cheese, crumbled
12 ounces smoked pork shoulder, pulled
1 tablespoon Texas Pete Hot Sauce®
1/4 cup thinly sliced pickled baby okra

Brush the baguette slices lightly with olive oil and season with salt and pepper. Arrange on a baking sheet and toast until crisp. Layer the slices with half the cheese, the smoked pork, several drops of hot sauce and the remaining cheese. Top each with two slices of pickled okra. *Serves 12*

This was served at the Savoring Flavors Event.

Fried Green Tomatoes with Boursin, Bacon and Chives

1 roasted yellow or red bell pepper
3 tablespoons chicken broth
4 ounces boursin cheese, softened
2 tablespoons cream cheese, softened
6 green tomatoes
1 cup all-purpose flour
1/2 cup cornmeal
1 tablespoon Cajun seasoning
1 teaspoon salt
1/2 teaspoon pepper
1 egg
1 cup buttermilk
1/4 cup vegetable oil
2 slices thick-cut bacon, crisp-cooked and chopped
1 tablespoon chopped fresh chives

Process the bell pepper with the broth in a blender or food processor, scraping the side frequently. Combine the boursin cheese and cream cheese in a bowl and mix until smooth.

Slice the green tomatoes 1/4 inch thick and cut each slice into halves. Mix the flour, cornmeal, Cajun seasoning, salt and pepper in a bowl. Blend the egg and buttermilk in a bowl. Dip each tomato slice into the egg mixture and then coat with the flour mixture.

Heat the oil in a heavy skillet. Add the breaded tomatoes and fry until golden brown on both sides. Drain and cool.

Spread the boursin cheese mixture on the tomato slices and top each with the bacon and chives. Arrange on a serving plate and drizzle with the roasted bell pepper sauce. *Serves 12*

Tomato and Fresh Mozzarella Napoleons with Flash-Fried Prawns

3 roma tomatoes
1 tablespoon julienned fresh basil
Salt and pepper to taste
16 ounces fresh mozzarella cheese (preferably handmade)
18 slices baguette
2 teaspoons extra-virgin olive oil
3 tablespoons all-purpose flour
3 tablespoons cornstarch
6 prawns, or 6 (12-count) jumbo shrimp, peeled and deveined

1 cup canola oil or peanut oil
6 tablespoons Alfredo Sauce (page 54)
2 lemons, peeled, sectioned and chopped
1/2 teaspoon sugar
1 teaspoon chopped parsley
6 tablespoons Balsamic Glaze (page 54)

Preheat the oven to 400 degrees. Slice the tomatoes into eighteen rounds about 1/4 inch thick; season with the basil, salt and pepper. Slice the mozzarella cheese and cut the cheese and baguette slices each into eighteen rounds the same circumference as the tomatoes. Drizzle the bread lightly with the olive oil and place on a baking sheet. Toast the bread lightly. Maintain the oven temperature.

Layer one slice of toasted bread, one slice of tomato and one slice of cheese in a stack. Repeat the layers until the stack is three layers high. Repeat the process with the remaining ingredients to make six Napoleons; align the stacks carefully on a greased baking sheet.

Mix the flour and cornstarch with salt and pepper in a bowl. Coat the prawns with the flour mixture. Heat the canola oil to 400 degrees and add the prawns. Fry for 1 to 2 minutes; drain.

Spoon 1 tablespoon of the Alfredo Sauce over each Napoleon. Bake for 5 to 8 minutes. Remove to a serving plate and top each with a prawn. Toss the lemon with the sugar and parsley and season with salt and pepper. Spoon over the shrimp and drizzle the stacks and plates with the Balsamic Glaze. *Serves 6*

Seared Ahi Tuna on Won Ton Crisps with Wasabi Whipped Cream and Soy Reduction

1/2 cup soy sauce
1/2 cup honey
6 won ton wrappers
2 cups peanut oil
Pinch of ground ginger
Salt and pepper to taste
12 ounces sashimi-grade tuna steak
1 1/2 tablespoons white sesame seeds
1 1/2 tablespoons black sesame seeds
1/2 cup heavy whipping cream
2 teaspoons wasabi powder
24 thin slices pickled ginger

Combine the soy sauce and honey in a small saucepan and simmer until reduced by half. Cool until slightly thickened.

Cut each won ton wrapper into four equal pieces for a total of twenty-four pieces. Reserve 1 teaspoon of the peanut oil to sear the tuna. Heat the remaining peanut oil in a saucepan until very hot. Add the won tons in batches and fry until crisp and golden brown. Drain and season with the ground ginger, salt and pepper.

Cut the tuna into rectangular or triangular pieces and season with salt and pepper. Mix the white sesame seeds and black sesame seeds in a shallow pan. Press the tuna into the seeds, coating both sides. Heat the reserved peanut oil in a skillet. Add the tuna and sear on both sides until the sesame seeds are golden brown but the tuna is still rare in the center. Cool for 20 minutes or longer. Whip the cream in a bowl until soft peaks form. Stir in the wasabi powder.

Slice the tuna into twenty-four pieces measuring about 3/4×3/4-inch. Place one piece of tuna on each won ton crisp and top each with a slice of pickled ginger. Add a dollop of wasabi whipped cream and drizzle with the soy sauce reduction.
Serves 12

This is an elegant hors d'oeuvre to pass or to serve on a buffet table.

Monique Darden
Brookridge Retirement Community

Monique Darden walked in to the TCK classroom on the first day full of energy, emotion and questions. For the first week it was unclear if she would be able to harness all of the emotion and turbulence in her life to focus on and succeed at the task at hand.

A single mother in her early twenties, Monique was spending a lot of time beating herself up for the bad decisions she had made in her past. She seemed to spend a lot of time in my office crying. She worried about how others perceived her, if she would be accepted by the class, about whether she could make it. Little by little she settled down into the daily routine of the kitchen. The repetitive act of chopping vegetables for hours seemed to sooth her with its tap-tap-tap of forged steel on the cutting board. She still made mistakes, and she still worried a lot, but it didn't seem to bother her as much or to be as sharp.

About her decision to enroll at TCK Monique says, "[It was the] Best decision I've ever made on my own. It allowed me to be where I really wanted to be, in culinary. I am so grateful for TCK because it allowed me to see where I could go, that I could work through mistakes and keep moving forward. I really enjoyed it."

Upon graduation Monique found a job at Forest Heights Retirement Community as a dietary aide. Though it wasn't cooking, it kept her close to the food end of things and provided some much needed income and stability. Then, after a year there, she was offered a job as a prep cook at Brookridge Retirement Community under chef Tom Peters, where she was able to work her way up to café cook.

As of 2011 she has been at Brookridge for over eighteen months. That, coupled with her time at Forest Heights, represents the longest uninterrupted period of employment in her life. She is planning to pursue a two-year culinary arts degree soon and says that nothing can stop her now from becoming a "real chef."

Grilled Chicken Salad

Dry Rub
1 1/2 tablespoons onion powder
1 tablespoon granulated garlic
1 tablespoon ground oregano
1 tablespoon dry tarragon
1 tablespoon seasoned salt
1 tablespoon lemon pepper
1/2 teaspoon black pepper

Chicken Salad
1 pound chicken tenders
1 head shredded iceberg lettuce
3/4 cup shredded carrots
2 cups diced tomatoes
1/2 cup diced red onion
1/2 cup finely chopped broccoli (optional)
1 cup (4 ounces) shredded Cheddar cheese
2 cups sliced cucumbers
3 eggs, hard-cooked and cut into quarters
2 or 3 sprigs of parsley

Rub: Combine the onion powder, granulated garlic, oregano, tarragon, seasoned salt, lemon pepper and black pepper in a small bowl; mix well.

Salad: Preheat the grill. Coat the chicken evenly with the Dry Rub. Grill the chicken until it reaches 165 degrees internally. Let rest for 5 minutes. Cut into slices. Layer the lettuce, carrots, tomatoes, onion, broccoli and cheese in a large salad bowl. Arrange the cucumber slices around the edge. Top with the sliced chicken, eggs and parsley. *Serves 8*

Monique Darden, Brookridge Retirement Community

Apricot Ginger Couscous

1 cup couscous
1 scallion, diced
1/2 cup finely diced dried apricots
1/4 cup soy sauce
1/4 cup rice vinegar
2 tablespoons sesame oil
1 tablespoon minced fresh ginger

Cook the couscous using the package directions; drain. Combine with the scallion, apricots, soy sauce, vinegar, sesame oil and ginger in a bowl; mix well. Chill slightly to serve. *Serves 6*

Asparagus and Spinach Salad with Raspberry Vinaigrette

Raspberry Vinaigrette
1/2 pint fresh raspberries
1/4 cup balsamic vinegar
2 teaspoons honey
1 teaspoon minced garlic
1/2 teaspoon Dijon mustard
Salt and pepper to taste
1/2 cup olive oil

Asparagus and Spinach Salad
Salt to taste
1 bunch fresh asparagus, trimmed and cut into 1-inch lengths
1 (6-ounce) package fresh baby spinach
1/2 pint fresh raspberries
1 carrot, shredded
1/2 cup toasted sliced almonds

Vinaigrette: Purée the raspberries in a blender. Add the vinegar, honey, garlic, Dijon mustard, salt and pepper and mix well. Add the olive oil gradually, blending constantly until smooth.

Salad: Bring a medium saucepan of salted water to a boil. Add the asparagus and cook for 5 to 7 minutes or just until tender. Plunge into ice water to stop the cooking process; drain well. Combine with the spinach, raspberries, carrot and almonds in a large salad bowl. Toss with the desired amount of vinaigrette to serve. *Serves 8*

Pam Browning

Fresh Mozzarella and Summer Strawberry Salad with Honey Balsamic Dressing

4 thin slices French bread
1 tablespoon olive oil
1/2 cup (2 ounces) shredded Parmesan cheese
16 ounces fresh mozzarella cheese
2 cucumbers, peeled
1 golden heirloom tomato
1 red tomato
1/2 cup diced yellow bell pepper
1/2 cup chopped walnuts
2 cups sliced strawberries
1 1/2 cups baby lettuce leaves
3/4 cup Honey Balsamic Dressing (page 60)

Preheat the oven to 325 degrees. Drizzle the bread slices with the olive oil and sprinkle with the Parmesan cheese. Place on a baking sheet and toast until crisp. Cut into triangles.

Slice the mozzarella cheese and then cut into 1/4-inch dice. Cut the cucumbers into halves lengthwise, scrape out the seeds and then cut into thin slices. Cut the golden tomato and red tomato into quarters and slice.

Combine the mozzarella cheese, cucumbers, tomatoes, bell pepper, walnuts, strawberries and lettuce in a large bowl. Add the Honey Balsamic Dressing and toss to coat evenly. Serve with the cheese toasts. *Serves 6*

Cara Cara Orange Salad with Fennel Vinaigrette, Pine Nuts, Ricotta Salata and Mint

Fennel Vinaigrette
2 tablespoons finely minced fennel bulb
1 1/2 tablespoons white wine vinegar
1 teaspoon sugar
3 tablespoons extra-virgin olive oil
Salt and white pepper to taste

Cara Cara Orange Salad
3 Cara Cara oranges or other navel oranges
2 tablespoons thinly julienned basil
2 tablespoons thinly julienned mint
2 tablespoons toasted pine nuts
2 tablespoons shaved ricotta salata
1 tablespoon extra-virgin olive oil

Vinaigrette: Mix the fennel, vinegar and sugar in a small bowl. Whisk in the olive oil and season with salt and white pepper. Let stand for 1 hour or longer.

Salad: Peel the oranges with a serrated knife, taking care to remove all the white pith. Cut each orange into eight thin slices. Combine the orange slices with the vinaigrette in a bowl, coating well.

Arrange four orange slices on each of six serving plates; drizzle with the dressing. Sprinkle with the basil, mint, pine nuts and ricotta cheese. Drizzle with the olive oil. *Serves 6*

Panzanella

1 cup bread cubes, toasted
3 cups diced fresh tomatoes
1 cup diced seeded cucumber
3/4 cup diced red bell pepper
3/4 cup diced yellow bell pepper
3/4 cup diced celery hearts

2 teaspoons minced garlic
3 tablespoons chopped fresh basil
2 tablespoons drained capers
1 1/4 cups Red Wine Vinaigrette
  (page 61)

Combine the bread cubes with the tomatoes, cucumber, bell peppers, celery and garlic in a bowl. Add the basil, capers and Red Wine Vinaigrette; mix well. Serve immediately. *Serves 10*

This rustic bread salad from the Tuscan region of Italy is especially good served in a bread bowl or Edible Parmesan Crisp Bowl (page 66).

Jicama Peach Slaw

3 tablespoons fresh lime juice
1 teaspoon grated lime zest
2 tablespoons honey
3/4 cup canola oil

2 cups julienned peeled jicama
2 cups julienned peeled firm peaches
2 tablespoons chopped fresh mint

Combine the lime juice, lime zest and honey in a food processor or blender. Add the canola oil gradually, processing constantly until smooth. Mix the jicama and peaches in a bowl. Add the mint and drizzle with the dressing; toss to coat evenly. Chill until serving time. *Serves 6*

This fresh and tangy salad is a great substitute for regular coleslaw.

Chef Pam's Potato Salad

Cooked Dressing
10 eggs
3/4 cup apple cider vinegar
1/2 cup sugar
2 to 4 drops yellow food coloring
1 1/2 cups mayonnaise

Potato Salad
5 pounds Yukon Gold potatoes
8 eggs
2 bunches scallions, finely diced
Salt and pepper to taste

Dressing: Whisk the eggs in a medium saucepan. Whisk in the vinegar, sugar and food coloring. Cook over medium-low heat until thickened, stirring constantly. Remove from the heat and stir in the mayonnaise.

Salad: Cook the unpeeled potatoes in boiling water in a saucepan until fork tender; drain. Cook the eggs in boiling water in a saucepan for 20 minutes; drain. Let the potatoes and eggs stand until cool enough to handle. Cut the potatoes into medium dice; slice the eggs or cut into small dice. Combine the potatoes, eggs and scallions in a bowl. Add the dressing and season with salt and pepper; mix gently. Chill in the refrigerator until serving time; flavors improve if chilled overnight. *Serves 16*

Pam Browning

Loaded Baked Potato Salad

4 cups diced baked white or red thin-skinned potatoes
1 cup (4 ounces) shredded sharp Cheddar cheese
1/2 cup sour cream
1/2 cup mayonnaise
1/2 cup chopped crisp-cooked bacon
2 tablespoons chopped chives
1 teaspoon salt
1/2 teaspoon coarsely ground pepper

Combine the potatoes, cheese, sour cream, mayonnaise, bacon, chives, salt and pepper in a bowl; mix well. Chill until serving time. *Serves 6*

A new twist on potato salad with a familiar theme.

Greek Orzo Salad

16 ounces orzo
10 ounces feta cheese, crumbled
2 ripe tomatoes, chopped
1 red bell pepper, diced
1/2 green bell pepper, diced
1/2 red onion, minced
1 tablespoon minced garlic
1/2 cup extra-virgin olive oil
2 tablespoons red wine vinegar
1 tablespoon lemon juice
1 tablespoon chopped fresh oregano
1 tablespoon chopped fresh basil
Salt and pepper to taste

Cook the pasta using the package directions; drain. Combine with the cheese, tomatoes, bell peppers, onion and garlic in a bowl. Add the olive oil, vinegar, lemon juice, oregano, basil, salt and pepper; mix well. Chill until serving time. *Serves 12*

Ed Williams
Winston-Salem State University

Edward Williams is soft spoken and polite. During his time in the Triad Community Kitchen Culinary Job Training Program, he diligently went about his business, never causing disruption or even speaking up much. Get Edward alone and in a conversation though, and you will quickly learn that this is a man with an acute opinion and view of the world and its injustices.

Inside of Ed Williams is a revolutionary. Held down by the low expectations of society and a series of dead-end jobs, Ed has nevertheless managed to publish several volumes of literature and poetry. Some of these works, especially the poetry, are what society would lump together in a category known as "Street Poetry," but there is more to it than that. Addressing societal issues with a clarity reminiscent of Richard Wright and with a poetic style similar to LeRoi Jones, (now known as Amiri Baraka), Ed can only hope to achieve in his cuisine what he has already done with his writing.

Employed at Winston-Salem State University in the Catering Division under Chef Derrick McCorkle since his graduation in July of 2007, Ed quickly worked his way up to supervisor of the Pastry and Baking Department. Chef McCorkle recalls, "We had an illness with our pastry chef, and we really didn't have a replacement available on staff. Edward wanted to try, so we threw him a recipe book and told him to study it. Through hard work he somehow managed to do it, and he's never looked back."

Edward has recently enrolled as a full-time culinary student at Guilford Technical Community College. His view on culinary education is, "When you get on the job there are some things that may take years to learn, but if you have the culinary education it lets you progress much faster than just learning through hands-on experience."

We are all expecting big things from a man who has already done big things. He sums up his determination by saying, "All my life I've been an underdog, but I've always maintained a positive attitude and believed that I could break out of the box people have placed me in. Now I'm out of that box."

Savory Rotini Salad

Wine Vinaigrette
1 1/2 cups olive oil
1 cup white balsamic vinegar
1/4 cup white wine
Grated zest of 2 oranges
1/4 cup fresh basil chiffonade
1 teaspoon minced fresh garlic
1 teaspoon Italian seasoning
1 teaspoon salt
1 teaspoon cracked pepper

Savory Rotini Salad
2 cups rotini
1 cup diced carrots
1 cup broccoli spears
2 large red onions
2 oranges, peeled
3/4 cup crumbled feta cheese
6 tablespoons dried cranberries

Vinaigrette: Combine the olive oil, vinegar, wine, orange zest, basil, garlic, Italian seasoning, salt and pepper in a bowl. Mix until smooth.

Salad: Cook the pasta using the package directions; rinse in cold water and drain. Blanch the carrots and broccoli in boiling water in a saucepan for 2 minutes. Plunge into a bowl of ice water to stop the cooking process; drain and pat dry. Cut the onions into halves and then into slices. Cut each orange into eight wedges. Combine the oranges with the pasta, carrots, broccoli and onions in a bowl. Add the vinaigrette and mix well. Chill for 2 hours or longer. Serve on chilled plates and top with the cheese and cranberries. *Serves 8*

Chef Derrick McCorkle and Edward Williams,
Winston-Salem State University

Seafood Pasta Salad

Zesty Dressing
1/2 cup white wine
2 tablespoons minced shallots
1 tablespoon lemon juice
1 1/2 teaspoons minced garlic
2 tablespoons Old Bay seasoning
1 tablespoon crushed red pepper
1 teaspoon kosher salt
1/2 teaspoon black pepper
1/2 cup olive oil
1/4 cup canola oil

Salad
4 cups water
1 (12-ounce) can beer
1 tablespoon lemon juice
3 tablespoons Old Bay seasoning
1 pound large shrimp, peeled and deveined
1 pound penne, cooked, drained and cooled
8 ounces jumbo lump crab meat
2 scallions, chopped
2 tomatoes, diced
2 cucumbers, peeled and diced
1 red bell pepper, diced
1/2 cup (4 ounces) shredded Parmesan cheese

Dressing: Combine the wine, shallots, lemon juice, garlic, Old Bay seasoning, crushed red pepper, kosher salt and black pepper in a bowl. Add the olive oil and canola oil in a steady stream, whisking constantly until emulsified. Store in the refrigerator.

Salad: Combine the water, beer, lemon juice and Old Bay seasoning in a large saucepan. Bring to a boil and add the shrimp. Cook just until the shrimp are pink and cooked through. Drain and cool the shrimp in a bowl of ice water; drain. Combine the shrimp with the pasta, crab meat, scallions, tomatoes, cucumbers and bell pepper in a bowl; mix well. Add the dressing and cheese and toss to coat evenly. Adjust the seasoning and chill in the refrigerator. *Serves 10*

Theme Adams

North Carolina Fresh Pico de Gallo

3 cups finely diced seeded tomatoes
2 jalapeño chiles, finely diced
1 Anaheim chile or other mild to medium chile, finely diced
1 cup finely diced sweet onion
1/2 cup chopped cilantro

1 teaspoon minced fresh garlic
3 tablespoons lime juice
1 tablespoon grated lime zest
2 tablespoons honey, or to taste
1 teaspoon salt, or to taste

Combine the tomatoes, jalapeño chiles, Anaheim chile, onion, cilantro and garlic in a bowl. Add the lime juice, lime zest, honey and salt; mix well. *Serves 12*

Far East Chopped Relish

1/2 cup finely diced pineapple
1/2 cup finely chopped bok choy
1/4 cup finely chopped green cabbage
1/4 cup finely chopped scallions
1/4 cup finely diced red bell pepper
1/2 teaspoon minced garlic
2 teaspoons soy sauce

2 teaspoons rice wine vinegar
1 teaspoon mirin
1 teaspoon minced fresh ginger
1/2 teaspoon sesame oil
1/4 teaspoon Sriracha hot sauce
1/4 teaspoon pepper

Combine the pineapple, bok choy, cabbage, scallions, bell pepper and garlic in a bowl. Add the soy sauce, vinegar, mirin, ginger, sesame oil, hot sauce and pepper; mix well. Chill in the refrigerator. Serve over grilled food or as a condiment for Asian dishes. *Serves 6*

Mango Guava Salsa

2 cups diced mango
1 cup diced guava
1 cup diced kiwifruit
1/2 cup diced red onion
1/2 cup diced yellow bell pepper
1/2 cup diced orange bell pepper
1/4 cup finely chopped cilantro
1/4 cup fresh lime juice
1/4 teaspoon cayenne pepper

Combine the mango, guava, kiwifruit, onion and bell peppers in a bowl. Add the cilantro, lime juice and cayenne pepper and mix well. Chill in the refrigerator for 1 hour or longer. *Serves 16*

William Webster

Tricks of the Trade

Triad Community Kitchen

Alfredo Sauce

3 garlic cloves, minced
2 tablespoons butter
6 cups heavy cream
1 cup chicken stock or chicken broth
1 tablespoon chicken bouillon granules or chicken base
1 teaspoon salt
1 tablespoon coarsely ground pepper
1/2 cup (2 ounces) grated Parmesan cheese

Sweat the garlic lightly in the melted butter in a saucepan. Add the cream, stock, chicken bouillon, salt and pepper; mix well. Bring to a simmer and cook until reduced to 5 1/2 cups and thickened enough to lightly coat the back of a metal spoon; stir occasionally. Remove from the heat and adjust the seasonings. Whisk in the Parmesan cheese. Serve immediately or cool to room temperature and store in an airtight container in the refrigerator. *Makes 6 cups*

Balsamic Glaze

1/2 cup balsamic vinegar
1/4 cup honey

Blend the vinegar and honey in a small saucepan and bring to a boil. Reduce the heat and cook until the mixture is reduced by one-half and coats the back of a spoon. *Makes 1/4 cup*

The glaze will continue to thicken as it cools.

Watermelon Barbecue Sauce

1/2 watermelon, red portion only, chopped
1/2 cup minced Vidalia onion
4 garlic cloves, minced
1 cup ketchup
1/2 cup honey
1/2 cup cider vinegar
1/2 cup Midori
2 tablespoons molasses
2 tablespoons teriyaki basting sauce and glaze
2 tablespoons brown sugar
2 tablespoons Texas Pete Hot Sauce®
1 tablespoon liquid smoke
1/2 teaspoon ancho chile powder
1/2 teaspoon chipotle chile powder
1/2 teaspoon cayenne pepper
Pinch each of allspice, ground cloves, cinnamon and ginger

Purée the watermelon. Press the purée through a sieve into a saucepan, discarding the solids. Add the onion and garlic. Bring to a simmer and simmer for 30 to 60 minutes or until reduced to 2 cups. Add the ketchup, honey, vinegar, liqueur, molasses, teriyaki basting sauce, brown sugar, hot sauce and liquid smoke. Stir in the ancho chile powder, chipotle chile, cayenne pepper, allspice, cloves, cinnamon and ginger. Return to a simmer and simmer for 20 minutes. Cool to room temperature to serve. *Makes 4 cups*

Blood Orange Sauce

2 tablespoons minced shallots
1 cup blood orange juice
1/3 cup raspberry vinegar
1/4 cup (1/2 stick) butter, cut into 1/4-inch slices
Salt and pepper to taste

Combine the shallots with the orange juice and vinegar in a saucepan. Cook until reduced to 1/4 cup or until thickened to the desired consistency. Remove from the heat and add the butter gradually, stirring until melted after each addition. Season with salt and pepper. *Makes 2/3 cup*

Serve with duck or game or with rich seafood, such as scallops or lobster.

Wild Game Bourbon Sauce

1 teaspoon minced garlic
1 teaspoon minced white onion
1 teaspoon minced shallot
1 teaspoon olive oil
1 1/3 cups packed dark brown sugar
1 cup pineapple juice
2/3 cup water
1/2 cup bourbon
1/4 cup teriyaki sauce
1/4 cup lemon juice
1/4 cup crushed pineapple
1/4 teaspoon cayenne pepper

Sauté the garlic, onion and shallot in the olive oil in a saucepan over low heat for 5 minutes. Add the brown sugar, pineapple juice, water, bourbon, teriyaki sauce, lemon juice, crushed pineapple and cayenne pepper; mix well. Reduce the heat and simmer for 35 to 45 minutes or until thickened to the desired consistency. *Makes 4 cups*

William Webster

Cajun Hollandaise Sauce

3 egg yolks, about 1/4 cup
1 1/2 teaspoons lemon juice
1/2 cup clarified butter
1 tablespoon marinara sauce
1 teaspoon Texas Pete Hot Sauce®
1 teaspoon Cajun seasoning
Salt to taste

Combine the egg yolks and lemon juice in a double boiler; mix well. Cook over simmering water just until the egg yolks turn bright yellow and begin to thicken, stirring constantly. Remove from the heat and beat in the butter until thickened. Stir in the marinara sauce, hot sauce, Cajun seasoning and salt. Serve immediately, discarding any unused sauce. For traditional Hollandaise sauce, omit the marinara sauce and Cajun seasoning. *Makes 3/4 cup*

Espagnole Sauce

1/2 cup diced onion
3 tablespoons vegetable oil
1/4 cup diced carrot
1/4 cup diced celery
2 tablespoons tomato paste

8 cups brown veal stock or
   beef stock, heated
3/4 cup brown roux
1 Sachet D'Epices (page 65)

Sauté the onion in the oil in a saucepan until light brown. Add the carrot and celery and sauté until light brown. Stir in the tomato paste and cook until medium brown. Add the stock and bring to a simmer. Whisk in the roux. Return to a simmer, stirring constantly. Add the Sachet D'Epices. Simmer for 1 hour, skimming the surface as needed. Strain through a double thickness of rinsed cheesecloth into a bowl. Serve immediately or cool to room temperature and store in the refrigerator. *Makes 8 cups*

Orange Sesame Glaze

3/4 cup Iron Chef Brand orange
   ginger sauce
1/2 cup mandarin orange sauce
1/2 cup teriyaki basting sauce
   and glaze
1/2 cup orange juice

1/4 cup soy sauce
1/4 cup water
2 tablespoons minced scallions
1 tablespoon minced fresh ginger
1 tablespoon sesame oil

Combine the orange ginger sauce, mandarin orange sauce, teriyaki basting sauce, orange juice, soy sauce and water in a bowl. Add the scallions, ginger and sesame oil; mix well. *Makes 3 cups*

Use as a dipping sauce, stir-fry sauce, or glaze for pork, beef, or chicken. You can find the orange ginger sauce, mandarin orange sauce, and teriyaki basting sauce and glaze in the Asian section of most grocery stores.

Demi-Glace

4 cups (or more) brown veal stock or beef stock
4 cups Espagnole Sauce (page 58)

   Combine the stock and Espagnole Sauce in a heavy saucepan. Simmer over low to medium heat until the mixture is reduced by one-half and has a velvety consistency and glossy sheen, skimming the surface and adding stock as needed. Strain into a bowl. Serve immediately or cool to room temperature and store in the refrigerator. *Makes 6 cups*

Classic Velouté

3 tablespoons clarified butter
2 tablespoons finely diced onion
1 tablespoon finely diced celery
1 tablespoon finely diced parsnip
1/4 cup all-purpose flour
4 1/4 cups chicken stock
1 Sachet D'Epices (page 65)
1/2 teaspoon salt
White pepper to taste

   Heat the clarified butter in a saucepan and add the onion, celery and parsnip. Sauté until the vegetables are tender. Stir in the flour and cook until very light brown, stirring constantly. Whisk in the stock gradually. Bring to a boil and cook until thickened, stirring constantly. Add the Sachet D'Epices and simmer for 30 minutes. Season with the salt and white pepper. Strain into a bowl. *Makes 5 cups*

Honey Balsamic Dressing

1 cup balsamic vinegar
3/4 cup honey
1 tablespoon Dijon mustard
1 garlic clove, minced
1 shallot, minced

1/2 teaspoon salt
1/4 teaspoon freshly ground pepper
1 cup (or less) extra-virgin olive oil
3/4 cup (or less) canola oil
1/4 cup chopped fresh basil

Combine the vinegar, honey, Dijon mustard, garlic, shallot, salt and pepper in a food processor. Process at medium to high speed to mix well. Add the olive oil and canola oil gradually, processing constantly until of the desired consistency. Combine with the basil in an airtight container. Chill in the refrigerator.
Makes 4 cups

Citrus Sherry Vinaigrette

1/2 cup sherry vinegar
2 tablespoons honey
2 tablespoons frozen orange juice concentrate, thawed
2 tablespoons Dijon mustard
1 tablespoon minced shallot

1 teaspoon minced garlic
1/2 teaspoon salt
1/4 teaspoon pepper
1 cup olive oil
1 tablespoon chopped fresh parsley
1 teaspoon minced fresh thyme

Combine the vinegar, honey, orange juice concentrate, Dijon mustard, shallot, garlic, salt and pepper in a food processor. Pulse just until mixed. Add the olive oil gradually, processing constantly until smooth. Combine with the parsley and thyme in an airtight container. Chill for 1 hour before serving. Shake well before serving if the mixture separates. *Makes 2 cups*

Red Wine Vinaigrette

1 cup red wine vinegar
2 shallots, minced
2 teaspoons Dijon mustard
2 cups olive oil
1 cup canola oil or other vegetable oil

2 teaspoons sugar
1 teaspoon salt
1/2 teaspoon pepper
3 tablespoons minced parsley

Combine the vinegar, shallots and Dijon mustard in a food processor. Add the olive oil and canola oil gradually, processing constantly until smooth. Season with the sugar, salt and pepper. Combine with the parsley in a bowl. Chill in the refrigerator. *Makes 3 cups*

Chipotle Mayonnaise

1 egg yolk
1 tablespoon brown mustard
1 tablespoon puréed chipotle
  chiles in adobo sauce
1 tablespoon lemon juice

1 tablespoon chopped parsley
2 teaspoons minced shallot
1/4 teaspoon salt
Pepper to taste
3/4 cup vegetable oil

Combine the egg yolk, brown mustard, chiles, lemon juice, parsley, shallot, salt and pepper in a food processor or blender. Process for 30 seconds. Add the oil gradually, processing constantly until thickened to mayonnaise consistency. Adjust the seasonings. Serve on the same day. *Makes 1 cup*

If you are concerned about using uncooked egg yolks, use egg yolks from eggs pasteurized in their shells, which are sold at some specialty food stores, or use an equivalent amount of pasteurized egg yolk substitute.

Basic Brine for Poultry or Pork

1 gallon (16 cups) water
1 cup sugar
1 cup salt

Combine the water, sugar and salt in a large container. Use to soak poultry or pork in the refrigerator for 24 to 48 hours. *Brines 1 turkey or large roast*

This is enough brine to accommodate a medium-size turkey. You can reduce the recipe by one-half for chicken or smaller roasts. For extra flavor, infuse the brine with sprigs of fresh herbs.

Brown Beef Stock

6 pounds beef bones
20 cups cold water
1 cup diced onion
1/2 cup diced celery
1/2 cup diced carrot
1 Sachet D'Epices (page 65)
Salt to taste

Preheat the oven to 350 degrees. Place the bones in a roasting pan. Roast until evenly caramelized. Combine the bones with the cold water in a large stockpot, deglazing the roasting pan with a portion of the water and adding it to the stockpot, if desired. Bring to a simmer and cook for 12 to 18 hours, skimming the surface as needed. Add the onion, celery, carrot and Sachet D'Epices. Simmer for 1 hour longer. Strain through a cheesecloth or fine-mesh strainer into a bowl; season with salt. Cool to room temperature. Store in the refrigerator. *Makes 1 gallon*

Basic Chicken Stock

6 pounds chicken bones, rinsed
20 cups cold water
1 cup diced onion
1/2 cup diced celery
1/2 cup diced carrot
1 Sachet D'Epices (page 65)

   Combine the chicken bones with the cold water in a large stockpot and bring to a boil. Reduce the heat to a simmer and simmer for 3 to 4 hours, skimming the surface as needed. Add the onion, celery and carrot. Simmer for 1 hour. Add the Sachet D'Epices and simmer for 30 minutes longer. Strain through a cheesecloth or fine-mesh strainer into a bowl. Cool to room temperature. Store in the refrigerator. *Makes 1 gallon*

Chipotle Dry Rub

1/2 cup packed brown sugar
1/2 cup chili powder
1/2 cup panko (Japanese bread crumbs)
1/4 cup onion powder
1/4 cup garlic powder
1/4 cup coarse salt
3 tablespoons pepper
2 tablespoons dry mustard
1 1/2 teaspoons chipotle chili powder

   Combine the brown sugar, chili powder, panko, onion powder, garlic powder, coarse salt, pepper, dry mustard and chipotle chili powder in a large bowl and mix well. Spoon into an airtight container. Store in the freezer for up to several months. *Makes 2 cups*

Pam Browning

Chef Jeff's Barbecue Rub

2 tablespoons brown sugar
1 tablespoon paprika
1 tablespoon kosher salt
1/2 tablespoon coarsely ground pepper
1/2 tablespoon granulated garlic
1/2 tablespoon onion powder
1/2 teaspoon chili powder
1/2 teaspoon cumin
1/4 teaspoon chipotle chili powder
1/4 teaspoon ancho chili powder
1/8 teaspoon ginger
1/8 teaspoon allspice

Combine the brown sugar, paprika, kosher salt and pepper in a bowl. Add the granulated garlic, onion powder, chili powder, cumin, chipotle chili powder, ancho chili powder, ginger and allspice and mix well. Store in an airtight container.
Makes 1/3 cup

This spicy/sweet concoction can be used for any barbecued or grilled food.

Cajun Seasoning

1/4 cup paprika
1/4 cup garlic powder
1/4 cup dried marjoram
1/4 cup dried thyme
2 tablespoons onion powder
1/4 cup salt
1/4 cup black pepper
3 tablespoons cayenne pepper

Combine the paprika, garlic powder, marjoram, thyme, onion powder, salt, black pepper and cayenne pepper in a bowl and mix well. Store in an airtight container. *Makes 1 3/4 cups*

Sachet D'Epices

3 sprigs of parsley
1 sprig of thyme, or 1/2 teaspoon dried thyme
1 garlic clove
1 bay leaf
1/2 teaspoon cracked peppercorns

Place the parsley, thyme, garlic, bay leaf and peppercorns on a square of cheesecloth and tie the cloth with kitchen twine to enclose the seasonings. *Makes 1 sachet*

Use to add a burst of herbal flavor to soup, stock, or sauce. Remove from the liquid before serving.

Edible Parmesan Crisp Bowls

2 1/2 cups (10 ounces) shredded Parmesan cheese

Preheat the oven to 350 degrees. Line four baking sheets with baking parchment. Sprinkle the Parmesan cheese into an 8- or 9-inch circle on each baking sheet. Bake for 7 to 12 minutes or until golden brown. Remove from the oven and drape immediately over a bowl or cup that is the size needed, pressing lightly to form the bowl. Cool until set. Store in an airtight container for up to 2 days.

For Parmesan Crisps, sprinkle the cheese in twelve 3-inch circles on the parchment-lined baking sheets and bake as above. Serve with salads and soups or as a snack. *Makes 4 bowls or 12 crisps*

Casual Comfort

Triad Community Kitchen

Lester Davis
WS Prime Restaurant

Lester Davis picked up a habit while serving in the army. It took awhile for this habit to totally destroy his life, but given enough time, addiction always achieves its goal.

Lester held a couple of jobs in Winston-Salem after his tour of duty, most notably at Atlantic Scrap and McCain Trucking, but from 1999 forward, his job was running the streets and finding ways to get more drugs. He initially had a roof over his head by staying with family members, but from 2005 to 2007 he was totally homeless.

In desperation he turned to Samaritan Ministries of Winston-Salem for shelter and food. Early on he learned about Project Cornerstone, a long-term residential treatment program that is offered at Samaritan Ministries. He saw it as a chance to save his life. From there, he never looked back. Through the partnership of the Second Harvest Food Bank of NWNC with Samaritan Ministries, Lester heard about the Triad Community Kitchen Culinary Training Program. His counselor suggested he consider it, and in October 2007 he enrolled.

After graduating with perfect attendance and being voted Most Valuable Teammate by his class, Lester secured an entry-level position at the Twin City Quarter Hotel and Convention complex in downtown Winston-Salem. He has continued his trend of perfect attendance and has received three raises and two promotions in his two-plus years at the Twin City Quarter under Chef Christian Froelich.

Lester says that his philosophy at work is, "I want everything I do to reflect positively on the Triad Community Kitchen. I ask myself, 'Is this how TCK would do it?' Then that's how I want to do it."

In 2009 Lester was selected as the Triad Community Kitchen's Graduate of the Year for 2008. He has also been honored by being chosen to come back as a keynote speaker at TCK graduations. His advice to others facing similar hurdles in life is, "Don't ever give up. Take the dream and run with it."

Braised Beef Ribs

1 (10-pound) rack of bone-in beef short ribs
Kosher salt and pepper to taste
1/4 cup olive oil
4 ribs celery, coarsely chopped
2 large yellow onions, cut into quarters
3 carrots, peeled and coarsely chopped
8 garlic cloves
1 (750-milliliter) bottle red wine
1/2 cup tomato paste
8 cups (or more) beef stock
10 bay leaves
1/2 cup chopped fresh thyme

Preheat the oven to 400 degrees. Slip a dull knife under a corner of the membrane on the whole rack of ribs and grasp with a dish towel or paper towel; pull to remove the membrane. Season both sides with kosher salt and pepper. Place the beef on a broiler pan. Roast for 20 to 30 minutes or until the beef is brown and the fat is rendered.

Heat the olive oil in a roasting pan until it begins to smoke. Add the celery, onions and carrots. Sauté until brown on all sides. Add the garlic and sauté for 30 seconds. Stir in the wine and tomato paste, taking care to avoid splatters. Bring to a simmer and then add the beef to the pan. Add enough stock to cover the beef; add the bay leaves and thyme. Cover tightly with a lid or foil. Reduce the oven temperature to 275 degrees. Roast the beef for 3 to 3 1/2 hours or until the meat is tender enough to pull from the bones using a fork, checking every 30 minutes after 2 hours and adding additional stock if the beef is less than two-thirds covered; do not overcook.

Remove the beef to a platter to cool. Strain the cooking liquid through a mesh strainer or cheesecloth, discarding the solids. Return the beef to the roasting pan and pour the strained liquid over the top. Chill in the liquid for 2 hours or longer.

Discard any fat that may have risen to the surface. Remove the beef and pour the liquid into a large saucepan; bring to a simmer. Cut the beef into servings between the ribs. Place in the saucepan and add additional stock if needed to keep the ribs moist. Simmer for 15 to 20 minutes or until the ribs reach 170 degrees internally and the sauce is slightly thickened. Thicken the sauce with a slurry of equal parts water and flour if needed for the desired consistency. Serve with your favorite starch and vegetables. *Serves 10 to 15*

Lester Davis, Winston-Salem Prime Restaurant

Texas Barbecued Beef Brisket

2 (3 1/2-pound) beef briskets
Chef Jeff's Barbecue Rub (page 64)
Watermelon Barbecue Sauce (page 55)

Trim any excess fat from the briskets and rub on all sides with Chef Jeff's Barbecue Rub. Let stand in the refrigerator for 24 hours. Soak oak, pecan, mesquite or hickory wood chips in a bowl of water for 24 hours.

Prepare a grill with real hardwood charcoal and heat with the lid closed until the coals are white-hot and register 250 degrees. Bank the coals to one side of the grill. Add the briskets fat side down away from the banked coals. Add a few of the soaked wood chips and close the lid. Grill for 4 to 5 hours or until fork-tender, turning every hour and adding additional charcoal and wood chips each time: maintain the heat at 225 to 250 degrees and keep the lid closed. Wrap the briskets in foil if they become too dark during the grilling process; the smoky flavor will be reduced, but it will prevent burning.

Remove the briskets to a platter and let rest for 30 minutes. Cut across the grain into thin slices. Serve with Watermelon Barbecue Sauce. *Serves 18*

You can prepare one brisket in the same manner if you prefer, or if your grill is small. Look for real hardwood charcoal in some supermarkets and most home-improvement stores.

Santa Maria-Style Barbecued Tri-Tip Beef Roast

Seasoning Salt
6 tablespoons salt
1/4 cup granulated garlic
2 teaspoons cayenne pepper
2 teaspoons white pepper
2 teaspoons freshly ground black pepper
1 teaspoon onion powder

Roast
1/2 cup red wine vinegar
1/2 cup vegetable oil
1 tablespoon Texas Pete Hot Sauce®
1 tablespoon minced garlic
1 (3-pound) tri-tip beef roast

Seasoning Salt: Combine the salt, granulated garlic, cayenne pepper, white pepper, black pepper and onion powder in a bowl; mix well.

Roast: Prepare a grill with real hardwood charcoal and add soaked oak chips; heat to low heat. Whisk the vinegar, oil, hot sauce and garlic in a small bowl. Coat the roast with half the Seasoning Salt. Let stand at room temperature for 30 minutes.

Place the roast fat side down on the grill. Grill for 6 to 8 minutes or until the first side becomes crisp, taking care to avoid flare-ups. Turn the roast and baste with the vinegar mixture; season lightly with the remaining Seasoning Salt. Grill until done to taste, turning four times; baste and season after each turn. Remove to a platter and let rest for 10 minutes. Cut across the grain into slices. *Serves 6*

Down Home Chili Beans with Beef

3 cups dried pinto beans
8 cups water
2 tablespoons beef bouillon granules
Salt and pepper to taste
1 1/4 pounds ground beef
1 cup diced onion
1/2 cup diced bell pepper
1 tablespoon minced garlic
2 cups canned diced tomatoes
1 cup tomato purée
1 cup ketchup
1/4 cup Texas Pete Hot Sauce®
2 tablespoons chili powder
1 tablespoon brown sugar
1 tablespoon cumin

Rinse and pick the beans. Combine with the water, beef bouillon, salt and pepper in a large saucepan. Cook for 2 hours. Brown the ground beef with the onion, bell pepper and garlic in a skillet, stirring until the ground beef is crumbly and the vegetables are tender; drain.

Add the tomatoes, tomato purée, ketchup, hot sauce, chili powder, brown sugar and cumin to the beans. Cook until heated through. Add the ground beef mixture and mix well. Simmer for 20 minutes or until heated to 165 degrees for 15 seconds or longer. *Serves 12*

Meat Sauce

2 pounds extra-lean ground beef
1 cup diced onion
1/4 cup diced green bell pepper
2 tablespoons minced garlic
1 tablespoon beef bouillon granules
6 cups tomato purée
1 cup canned diced tomatoes
1 cup water
2 tablespoons Italian seasoning
1 tablespoon sugar
1 tablespoon salt

Cook the ground beef, onion, bell pepper and garlic in a saucepan over low heat until the ground beef is crumbly and the vegetables are tender; drain. Add the beef bouillon. Stir in the tomato purée, tomatoes, water, Italian seasoning, sugar and salt. Simmer for 30 to 60 minutes or until done to taste. Adjust the seasonings. *Makes 3 quarts*

Barbecued Pork Ribs with Watermelon Barbecue Sauce

3 racks St. Louis-cut spareribs (about 4 pounds)
Chef Jeff's Barbecue Rub (page 64)
Watermelon Barbecue Sauce (page 55)

    Preheat the oven to 300 degrees. Slip a dull knife under a corner of the membrane on each rack of ribs and pull to remove the membrane. Rub the ribs generously with Chef Jeff's Barbecue Rub. Place each rack on a 15- to 18-inch-long sheet of extra-wide foil; fold the long edges over the ribs and seal tightly without allowing the foil to touch the ribs. Fold the ends over and seal, checking for any punctures.
    Place on a baking sheet. Roast for 3 hours or until very tender; a bone should start to separate from the meat when pulled. Roast longer if needed for tenderness, testing every 30 minutes. Remove from the oven and open the foil carefully; let stand for several minutes. Remove to a rack to cool completely.
    Heat a grill until hot. Coat the ribs generously on both sides with Watermelon Barbecue Sauce and grill until the surface is caramelized. Cut into individual servings. *Serves 6*

This is a home-kitchen version of barbecued ribs that is better than the pro's.

Red Beans and Rice

2 cups dried red beans
12 cups (or more) water
1 ham hock
1/4 cup chicken bouillon granules
1 cup diced yellow onion
2 garlic cloves, minced
Vegetable oil

1 tablespoon Texas Pete Hot Sauce®
1 tablespoon Cajun seasoning
Salt and pepper to taste
5 cups cooked white rice
1 pound smoked andouille, grilled or baked and sliced

    Rinse and pick the beans. Combine with enough water to cover in a bowl and let stand overnight; drain. Combine the beans with 12 cups water in a stockpot and bring to a boil. Reduce the heat to a light simmer and add the ham hock and chicken bouillon.

(continued)

Sauté the onion and garlic in a small amount of oil in a skillet. Add to the beans. Simmer for about 2 hours or just until the beans are tender and the cooking liquid is thick and creamy, adding water as needed for the desired consistency. Stir in the hot sauce, Cajun seasoning, salt and pepper. Discard the ham hock. Serve the beans over the rice in bowls and top with the sausage. *Serves 10*

Chicken and Dumplings

1 (3-pound) stewing chicken
1/4 cup chicken bouillon granules
10 cups water, boiling
2 eggs

1 cup all-purpose flour
Salt to taste
1 tablespoon margarine
White pepper to taste

Add the chicken and chicken bouillon to the boiling water in a large stockpot. Boil until the chicken is cooked through. Remove the chicken from the broth and cool the chicken and broth. Remove the meat from the bones, discarding the skin and bones. Strain the broth into a large saucepan.

Beat the eggs in a mixing bowl. Add the flour, salt and 1/2 cup of the reserved broth gradually, mixing to form a firm dough. Roll the dough in batches to 1/8-inch thickness on a floured surface. Cut into strips.

Return the remaining broth to a boil. Add the dough strips, stirring to prevent sticking. Return to a simmer and cook for 30 minutes. Stir in the chicken, margarine and white pepper and cook just until heated through. You can prepare the chicken and dough strips and store in the refrigerator until time to cook. *Serves 12*

Italian Cheese Chicken

Mushroom Sauce
1/3 cup butter
1/4 cup olive oil
1/2 cup finely diced onion
1/4 cup finely diced celery
1 tablespoon minced garlic
1 tablespoon dried oregano
1 3/4 cups finely diced mushrooms
1 cup baby portobellos
1/2 cup all-purpose flour
6 cups chicken stock
1/2 cup heavy cream
2 cups sour cream
1 cup (4 ounces) grated
   Parmesan cheese

Italian Cheese Chicken
2 cups panko (Japanese
   bread crumbs)
1 cup (4 ounces) grated
   Parmesan cheese
2 teaspoons dried oregano
12 boneless skinless chicken breasts
1/2 cup olive oil
1 cup (4 ounces) grated
   Parmesan cheese

Sauce: Heat the butter with the olive oil in a large saucepan over medium-high heat. Add the onion and celery and sauté for 5 minutes or until tender. Add the garlic and oregano and sauté for 5 minutes. Add the mushrooms and sauté for 3 minutes longer. Stir in the flour and cook until thickened and light brown, stirring constantly. Stir in the stock, heavy cream, sour cream and cheese; bring to a boil. Reduce the heat and simmer for 15 to 20 minutes.

Chicken: Preheat the oven to 350 degrees. Mix the panko, 1 cup cheese and the oregano in a bowl. Dip the chicken in the olive oil in a shallow dish and roll in the panko mixture, pressing to coat well. Arrange on a baking sheet. Bake for 30 minutes or to 145 degrees internally. Spread a layer of the mushroom sauce in a 9×13-inch baking dish. Arrange the chicken in the dish and top with the remaining sauce. Bake for 10 to 15 minutes or to 165 degrees internally. Sprinkle with 1 cup cheese and bake for 5 to 10 minutes longer or until the cheese is golden brown. *Serves 12*

Pam Browning

Four-Cheese Chicken Lasagna

Creamy Sauce
1/4 cup diced onion
1/4 cup diced bell pepper
1/2 cup (1 stick) butter
2 teaspoons minced garlic
2 teaspoons dried oregano
2 teaspoons dried basil
1/4 cup all-purpose flour
8 cups milk
2 cups chicken stock or chicken broth
2 cups diced cooked chicken breasts
1 cup (4 ounces) grated Parmesan cheese
1 (4-ounce) can sliced mushrooms, drained
1/4 cup chopped oil-pack sun-dried tomatoes

Four-Cheese Chicken Lasagna
1 (16-ounce) package lasagna noodles, cooked and drained
8 ounces ricotta cheese
3 cups (12 ounces) shredded Cheddar cheese
3 cups (12 ounces) shredded mozzarella cheese
1 cup (4 ounces) grated Parmesan cheese

Sauce: Sauté the onion and bell pepper in the butter in a 6- to 8-quart saucepan until transparent. Add the garlic, oregano and basil. Sauté for 2 to 3 minutes longer. Stir in the flour and cook for 2 to 3 minutes, stirring constantly. Whisk in the milk and stock. Cook until thickened and creamy, whisking constantly. Remove from the heat and add the chicken, cheese, mushrooms and sun-dried tomatoes.

Lasagna: Preheat the oven to 350 degrees. Arrange a layer of the noodles in a deep 9×13-inch baking pan sprayed with nonstick cooking spray. Layer half the ricotta cheese, one-third of the Cheddar cheese and one-third of the mozzarella cheese over the noodles. Top with one-third of the sauce. Repeat the layers. Add a last layer of noodles and top with the remaining sauce. Cover the layers with foil and bake for 30 to 45 minutes. Top with the remaining Cheddar cheese, mozzarella cheese and Parmesan cheese. Bake for 15 to 20 minutes longer or until the cheese is melted and light brown. Let stand for 10 minutes before serving. *Serves 12*

Pam Browning

Turkey Potpie Casserole

3 pounds turkey
10 cups water, boiling
1 egg
3/4 cup all-purpose flour
1/2 teaspoon salt
2 tablespoons chicken bouillon granules
1/2 cup diced onion
1 cup frozen mixed vegetables
2 tablespoons margarine
1/4 teaspoon white pepper
2 tablespoons cornstarch
2 tablespoons water

   Add the turkey to 10 cups boiling water in a large saucepan. Boil until the turkey is cooked through. Remove from the broth and cool the broth and turkey. Remove the turkey meat from the bones, discarding the skin and bones. Strain the broth back into the saucepan.
   Beat the egg in a mixing bowl. Add the flour, salt and 1/4 cup of the reserved broth gradually, mixing to form a firm dough. Roll the dough in batches to 1/8-inch thickness on a floured surface. Cut into strips.
   Bring the remaining broth to a boil in the saucepan and add the chicken bouillon. Add the onion and dough strips, stirring to prevent sticking. Return to a simmer and stir in the frozen vegetables, margarine and white pepper. Cook for 30 minutes. Thicken with a slurry of the cornstarch and 2 tablespoons water, stirring constantly. Stir in the turkey and heat to serving temperature.
Serves 12

Pasta Primavera

2 tablespoons olive oil
2 tablespoons minced shallots
1 teaspoon minced garlic
1/2 cup sliced yellow squash
1/2 cup sliced zucchini
1/2 cup diced red bell pepper
1/4 cup white wine
1/2 cup chicken broth
3 cups cream
1 cup blanched broccoli florets

1 cup blanched sliced carrots
1/2 cup quartered mushrooms
1 teaspoon salt
1/2 teaspoon pepper
3 cups pasta, cooked
1 teaspoon chopped fresh marjoram
1 teaspoon chopped fresh oregano
1/2 teaspoon chopped fresh thyme
1 tablespoon grated Parmesan cheese

   Heat the olive oil in a large saucepan. Add the shallots and garlic and sauté lightly. Add the yellow squash, zucchini and bell pepper; sauté for 30 seconds. Stir in the wine and cook until slightly reduced. Add the broth and cream and simmer for 30 seconds. Stir in the broccoli, carrots and mushrooms; simmer until the sauce begins to thicken. Season with the salt and pepper. Add the pasta, marjoram, oregano and thyme; toss to mix well. Serve hot immediately, topped with the cheese. *Serves 4*

You should have the ingredients for this dish measured and assembled before you begin. Add protein if desired by adding cooked chicken, shrimp, scallops or other seafood.

Pasta Vegetable Medley

1 cup chopped broccoli
1 cup chopped cauliflower
3 tablespoons olive oil
1 cup diced tomato
1 tablespoon minced garlic
1 cup sliced mushrooms
1/2 cup diced onion
1/2 cup diced bell pepper
2 tablespoons chopped fresh herbs (optional)
1 teaspoon salt
1/2 teaspoon pepper
2 cups pasta, cooked

Sauté the broccoli and cauliflower in the heated olive oil in a large saucepan for 7 minutes. Add the tomato and garlic and sauté for 5 minutes longer. Stir in the mushrooms, onion, bell pepper, herbs, salt and pepper. Add the pasta and toss to coat evenly. Adjust the seasonings and serve with freshly grated Parmesan cheese on the side. Add cooked chicken or seafood, if desired. *Serves 6*

Mediterranean Squash Blend with Pasta

2 cups penne
Olive oil for the pasta
3 tablespoons olive oil
1/2 cup finely diced onion
2 tablespoons minced garlic
1/2 teaspoon crushed red pepper flakes
1 cup finely diced yellow squash
1 cup finely diced zucchini
1 cup finely diced eggplant
1 (12-ounce) jar roasted red peppers, drained and finely diced
1 (15-ounce) can diced tomatoes
1/2 cup sliced black olives
2 teaspoons chopped fresh basil
2 teaspoons chopped fresh oregano
4 ounces feta cheese, crumbled
Salt and pepper to taste

Cook the pasta using the package directions; rinse with cold water and drain. Stir in a small amount of olive oil to prevent sticking.

Heat 3 tablespoons olive oil in a sauté pan over medium-high heat. Add the onion and sauté for 5 minutes. Add the garlic and red pepper flakes; sauté for 3 minutes. Add the yellow squash, zucchini, eggplant and roasted peppers and sauté until the vegetables are tender-crisp. Stir in the tomatoes, black olives, basil, oregano and pasta. Cook for 1 to 2 minutes. Add the cheese and toss just until the cheese begins to melt. Season with salt and pepper. *Serves 8*

Pam Browning

Barbecued Baked Beans

2 (28-ounce) cans baked beans
1/2 cup each minced bell pepper,
   carrots and celery
1/4 cup minced onion
3/4 cup packed brown sugar
1/4 cup chili powder
1 tablespoon garlic powder
1 tablespoon onion powder
1 tablespoon Texas Pete Hot Sauce®
1 teaspoon paprika
1/4 teaspoon cinnamon
1/4 teaspoon ground cumin
1/2 teaspoon salt
1/2 teaspoon pepper
1 pound bacon, crisp-cooked and
   crumbled, optional

Preheat the oven to 350 degrees. Combine the beans with the bell pepper, carrots, celery and onion in a bowl. Mix the brown sugar, chili powder, garlic powder, onion powder, hot sauce, paprika, cinnamon, cumin, salt and pepper in a small bowl. Add to the bean mixture and mix well. Spoon into a 9×13-inch baking pan. Bake for 1 hour. Top with the bacon. *Serves 12*

William Webster

Chef Pam's Collard Greens

2 bunches fresh collard greens
4 slices applewood-smoked bacon,
   finely diced
1/2 cup finely diced red onion
2 teaspoons minced garlic
1 teaspoon crushed red pepper flakes
1/4 cup white wine
1/4 cup apple cider vinegar
1 teaspoon sugar
1 teaspoon coarse salt
1 teaspoon restaurant-grind pepper

Wash the greens and cut out the stems. Roll the leaves tightly and cut crosswise into very thin strips. Render the bacon in a large sauté pan until brown and crisp. Add the onion, garlic and red pepper flakes; sauté for 5 minutes. Stir in the wine and vinegar and cook for 5 minutes. Add the greens and simmer for 15 to 20 minutes. Season with the sugar, salt and pepper. *Serves 5*

Pam Browning

Sweet Potato Casserole

5 to 6 cups mashed cooked
 sweet potatoes (about 6)
2 1/2 tablespoons powdered milk
2 cups water
1 1/2 cups sugar
1 egg
1/2 cup (1 stick) margarine
1/4 cup all-purpose flour
1/2 tablespoon lemon juice
2 teaspoons baking soda
Dash of nutmeg
Cinnamon to taste
1/4 teaspoon lemon extract
Marshmallows

Preheat the oven to 300 degrees. Combine sweet potatoes with the powdered milk, water, sugar, egg, margarine, flour, lemon juice, baking soda, nutmeg, cinnamon and lemon extract in a mixing bowl; mix until smooth. Spoon into a greased 9×13-inch baking pan. Bake for 45 to 50 minutes or until bubbly. Top with marshmallows and bake for 2 to 4 minutes longer or just until the marshmallows begin to brown. *Serves 12*

Coconut Rice

3 cups white rice
3 cups unsweetened coconut water
3 cups water
2 sprigs of fresh thyme
2 teaspoons salt

Combine the rice, coconut water, water, thyme and salt in a medium saucepan and bring to a boil. Reduce the heat and simmer until the first grains of rice float to the surface; do not stir. Cover tightly and remove from the heat. Let stand for 10 to 20 minutes or until the liquid is absorbed and the rice is tender. *Serves 12*

Coconut water is available in most Latin grocery stores. It is very important to use unsweetened coconut water for this rice. Alternately, you can crack open a fresh coconut or two for the water.

Mexican Corn Bread

1/2 cup finely diced purple onion
1/2 cup corn
1/4 cup canned minced jalapeño chiles
1 1/2 cups yellow cornmeal
1 1/4 cups all-purpose flour
3 tablespoons sugar
2 tablespoons baking powder
1 1/2 teaspoons salt
2 eggs, beaten
1 1/4 cups milk
1/4 cup shortening, melted and cooled
2 tablespoons Texas Pete Hot Sauce®
1 cup (4 ounces) shredded Cheddar cheese
1 tablespoon puréed canned chipotle chiles in adobo sauce

Preheat the oven to 350 degrees. Sauté the onion in a nonstick skillet until tender. Add the corn and jalapeño chiles and sauté just until heated through. Combine the cornmeal, flour, sugar, baking powder and salt in the bowl of a mixer fitted with the flat beater; mix well.

Combine the eggs, milk, shortening and hot sauce in a bowl and mix well. Add to the dry ingredients and mix at low speed just until moistened. Stir in the sautéed vegetables, cheese and puréed chiles. Spoon into a greased 9×9-inch baking pan. Bake for 35 minutes. *Serves 12*

Buttermilk Biscuits

2 cups all-purpose flour
2 tablespoons baking powder
2 tablespoons baking soda

1/2 tablespoon salt
1/2 cup shortening
1 cup buttermilk

Preheat the oven to 425 degrees. Whisk the flour with the baking powder, baking soda and salt in a bowl. Add the shortening and rub together until the mixture has the consistency of coarse cornmeal, scraping the bowl as needed. Add the buttermilk and mix by hand just until a dough forms. Knead lightly one to three times on a lightly floured surface. Roll 3/4 inch thick; dough will double in height as it bakes. Cut with a 2- to 2 1/2-inch round cutter; or cut into 2-inch squares with a knife. Place 1/2 inch apart on an ungreased baking sheet for crusty biscuits, or with sides touching for softer biscuits. Bake for 15 minutes or until golden brown. Space circular cuts close together to minimize scraps. Cutting with a roller cutter or cutting into squares reduces scraps. Scraps can be rerolled, but the biscuits may not be as tender. *Serves 10*

- For Sugared Biscuits, top each biscuit with 1/2 teaspoon sugar before baking.
- For Cheese Biscuits, reduce the shortening to 1/4 cup and add 1 cup shredded Cheddar cheese.
- For Whole Wheat Biscuits, substitute whole wheat flour for the all-purpose flour.
- For Butterscotch Biscuits, divide the dough into eight portions. Roll each portion into a rectangle 1/4 inch thick. Spread with melted margarine or butter and sprinkle with brown sugar. Roll to enclose the filling and cut into slices 3/4 inch thick. Bake at 375 degrees for 15 minutes.
- For Orange Biscuits, prepare as for Butterscotch Biscuits, substituting orange marmalade for the butter and brown sugar.
- For Cinnamon Raisin Biscuits, add 2 tablespoons sugar and 1/2 teaspoon cinnamon to the dry ingredients. Substitute margarine for the shortening and add 1/2 cup raisins to the dough after the margarine has been added. Ice baked biscuits with confectioners' sugar glaze.
- For Raisin Biscuits, reduce the buttermilk to 3/4 cup and increase the shortening to 3/4 cup. Add 2 beaten eggs, 1/2 cup sugar, 1/2 cup chopped raisins and 1 tablespoon grated orange zest.
- For Scotch Scones, add 2/3 cup sugar and 1/2 cup currants to the dry ingredients. Mix in 2 beaten eggs with the buttermilk. Cut the dough into squares and then into triangles. Brush lightly with milk before baking.

Big Night Out

Triad Community Kitchen

Vanessa Lanier
High Point Country Club

Vanessa Lanier sent me this e-mail in an effort to enroll in TCK, June 2007:

My name is Vanessa Lanier, and I am writing with a humble and desperate request.

I have never worked nor cooked in a professional kitchen. I am not a Chef nor am I an expert on the field, but I do know deep down, at the core of my being, that cooking is what I want to do. I believe that great cooking is in your soul or it isn't. I understand how valuable efficiency of movement is to minimize wasted energy and time; how important it is to value speed with precision, especially when knives, scalding oil, and hot steel are involved. I am firm believer of mental flexibility, as there is very little that cannot be accomplished if you set your mind to it. The implicit obligation of presenting your best.

I can work hard, very hard. I don't complain, I don't get tired, and I show up, no matter what. There is nothing that could stop me from reaching your kitchen when I am expected to be there. My life has been very, very hard, and I have two girls to care for. For some reason, since I was a little girl, my life has been about surviving one day after another, but I am smart, Chef Jeff. I have what it takes; I just need a chance, a chance to turn my life around, a chance to better myself. I have never been given anything, and quickly learned to ask for nothing. My father was shot when I was six years old in front of my brother and I, my mother essentially could no longer take care of us, so we were put in different homes, schools; life just got to be something else. I lived under men's rules and abuse just to keep a roof over my head, but I can no longer do that. I don't have anything to call my own, and I have felt pain in ways I never knew existed. My kids have suffered enough. My life is too crude for anyone to understand its depth. So, I am writing to you. I have a deep sense of respect and love for food and cooking, perhaps because I have always struggled to simply eat. I won't take any more of your time. Thank you for your time, and I hope to hear from you, chef.

Respectfully, Vanessa Lanier.

Vanessa graduated in October 2007 without missing a day of class and has worked as a line chef at High Point Country Club under Chef Eric Kirkeeng ever since. She has become proficient in all of the stations of the line and has aspirations to be a Certified Executive Chef one day. She works with two other TCK alumni at HPCC, Scott Randell and Mark Joyce. Vanessa was promoted to Executive Chef of Sapona Country Club in Lexington, NC, in January 2011.

Crispy Grilled Duck Breasts with Pan-Caramelized Local Peaches, White Asparagus and Port Reduction

3 fresh local peaches, cut into halves
3 tablespoons sugar
1 (750-milliliter) bottle port
2 tablespoons Demi-Glace (page 59) or brown sauce
6 (6-ounce) skin-on duck breasts
Salt and pepper to taste
8 ounces white asparagus, blanched

Place the peaches cut side down in the sugar on a plate; let stand for several hours.

Cook the wine in a saucepan until reduced to glaze consistency, adding the Demi-Glace halfway through the process; keep warm.

Preheat the grill to hot. Score the duck skin in a crisscross pattern; season on both sides with salt and pepper. Grill until medium-rare and remove from the grill; the duck will continue to cook to medium.

Sear the peaches in a sauté pan until caramelized. Sauté the asparagus lightly in a nonstick sauté pan. Slice the duck diagonally. Arrange the peaches, asparagus and duck evenly on serving plates; drizzle with the wine reduction. *Serves 6*

Vanessa Lanier, Scott Randell, and Mark Joyce, High Point Country Club

Garlic-Crusted Chicken Breasts with Summer Butter Sauce

1/2 cup oil-pack sun-dried tomatoes or dry-pack sun-dried tomatoes
4 slices crusty rolls or bread, toasted
1/4 cup (1 ounce) freshly grated Parmesan cheese
1/4 cup chopped fresh parsley
2 garlic cloves, minced
1 teaspoon salt
1/2 teaspoon freshly ground pepper
2 eggs
1/2 cup water
6 (6-ounce) boneless skinless chicken breasts
2 cups all-purpose flour
1/4 cup vegetable oil
1 cup white wine
2 shallots, minced
1/4 cup chopped fresh parsley
2 tablespoons lemon juice
1 cup (2 sticks) butter, sliced

Preheat the oven to 350 degrees. Soak the sun-dried tomatoes in enough warm water to cover in a bowl for 1 hour; drain. Combine the toasted bread with the cheese, 1/4 cup parsley, the garlic, salt and pepper in a food processor; process to form coarse crumbs. Beat the eggs with the water in a bowl.

Pound the chicken slightly less than 1/2 inch thick. Coat with the flour, dip in the egg mixture and then coat with the crumb mixture. Sauté in the oil in an ovenproof sauté pan until golden brown on both sides. Bake for 7 minutes or until cooked through.

Combine the wine and shallots in a shallow saucepan and cook until reduced to 1/2 cup. Remove from the heat and add the sun-dried tomatoes and 1/4 cup parsley. Stir in the lemon juice and remove from the heat. Add the butter, stirring until well mixed and slightly thickened. Adjust the seasonings.

Slice the chicken and arrange on serving plates. Top with the butter sauce.
Serves 6

Sautéed Chicken with Garden Herb Cream Sauce and Julienned Vegetables

6 (6-ounce) boneless skinless
   chicken breasts
Salt and pepper to taste
2 tablespoons vegetable oil
3/4 cup julienned carrot
3/4 cup julienned yellow bell pepper
3/4 cup julienned celery

1 shallot, minced
1/4 cup white wine
1 cup cream
2 tablespoons chopped fresh tarragon
2 tablespoons chopped fresh parsley
2 tablespoons chopped fresh basil
2 tablespoons chopped fresh chives

Preheat the oven to 200 degrees. Season the chicken with salt and pepper. Heat the oil in a sauté pan to just below the smoking point. Add the chicken and sauté for 2 minutes on each side or until golden brown on both sides. Remove to a baking sheet and keep warm in the oven; reserve the drippings in the sauté pan.

Steam the carrot, bell pepper, celery and shallot in a small amount of water in a covered container for 1 1/2 minutes in the microwave or just until tender-crisp. Add the wine to the reserved drippings in the sauté pan, stirring up any browned bits from the bottom. Add the cream and simmer until slightly thickened. Season with salt and pepper and stir in the tarragon, parsley, basil and chives. Spoon onto serving plates. Slice the chicken and place in the sauce; top with the steamed vegetables. *Serves 6*

Sautéed Chicken with Peaches, Country Ham and Black Pepper Triple Sec Cream

1 cup all-purpose flour
1 teaspoon salt
1/2 teaspoon pepper
6 (8-ounce French-cut) skin-on chicken breasts
1/2 cup clarified butter
1/2 cup julienned country ham
1/2 cup Triple Sec
1 cup heavy cream
2 cups diced peeled peaches
1 teaspoon coarsely ground pepper
Chopped fresh parsley and additional diced peaches,
   for garnish

Mix the flour, salt and pepper. Coat the chicken with the flour mixture, shaking off any excess. Heat the clarified butter in a skillet. Add the chicken skin side down and sauté until brown on both sides. Add the ham toward the end of the sautéing process and sauté until the ham begins to caramelize.

Pour off any excess or overbrowned drippings from the skillet. Add the liqueur, stirring to deglaze the skillet. Ignite the liqueur carefully and allow the flames to subside. Add the cream, 2 cups peaches and the coarsely ground pepper. Cook until reduced to the desired thickness.

Use tongs to place the chicken on serving plates. Top with the peaches and ham; pour the sauce over the top. Garnish with parsley and additional peaches. *Serves 6*

Shark Fin Chicken with Rum Basil Cream Sauce

Shark Fin Chicken
1 tablespoon Caribbean jerk seasoning
1 teaspoon garlic powder
1 teaspoon onion powder
1/2 teaspoon paprika
1/2 teaspoon pepper
1/4 teaspoon cinnamon
1/4 teaspoon salt
1/2 cup dark rum
1/2 teaspoon lime juice
1/2 teaspoon lemon juice
6 boneless chicken breasts
1 tablespoon vegetable oil

Rum Basil Cream Sauce
1/2 cup (1 stick) butter
1 tablespoon vegetable oil
1/2 cup chopped carrots
1/2 cup chopped celery
1/4 cup chopped onion
1 tablespoon all-purpose flour
1 cup chicken broth
1/2 cup dark rum
1/2 cup heavy cream
1 1/2 tablespoons chopped fresh basil
1 teaspoon grated lemon zest
1/2 teaspoon grated lime zest

Chicken: Mix the jerk seasoning, garlic powder, onion powder, paprika, pepper, cinnamon and salt in a large bowl. Stir in the rum, lime juice and lemon juice. Add the chicken and marinate in the refrigerator for 1 hour or longer.

Drain the chicken and pat dry. Sauté in the oil in a sauté pan until brown on both sides and 165 degrees internally.

Sauce: Melt the butter with the oil in a saucepan. Add the carrot, celery and onion. Sauté until the onion is translucent. Stir in the flour and cook for 1 minute or longer. Stir in the rum and broth and reduce the heat. Simmer for 5 to 10 minutes or until thickened, stirring constantly. Strain and return to the saucepan. Add the cream, basil, lemon zest and lime zest; mix well. Arrange the chicken on serving plates and top evenly with the sauce. *Serves 6*

William Webster

Coq au Vin

4 cups pearl onions
2 tablespoons minced garlic
1/4 cup olive oil
3 cups button mushrooms
2 cups red wine
1/2 cup diced bacon
6 pounds chicken leg quarters

2 cups chicken broth
1/4 cup cognac
1 bay leaf
2 tablespoons minced parsley
Salt and pepper to taste
1/2 cup (1 stick) butter
1/2 cup all-purpose flour

Sauté the onions and garlic in the olive oil in a sauté pan until tender. Add the mushrooms and sauté just until the mushrooms are tender. Remove the vegetables to a bowl with a slotted spoon, reserving the drippings in the pan. Add a small amount of the wine to the sauté pan, stirring to deglaze the pan. Pour over the vegetables.

Add the bacon to the sauté pan and render until the fat is translucent; remove the bacon with a slotted spoon, reserving the drippings in the pan. Add the chicken to the pan and sauté until brown.

Add the remaining wine, the broth, Cognac, bay leaf, parsley, salt and pepper, stirring to deglaze the pan. Simmer, covered, for 1 hour or until the chicken is tender.

Melt the butter in a skillet and stir in the flour. Cook until light brown, stirring constantly. Add to the chicken in the sauté pan and cook until thickened, stirring constantly. Simmer for 5 to 10 minutes longer. Add the vegetable mixture and simmer until heated through. Place the chicken on serving plates and spoon the sauce over the top, discarding the bay leaf. Sprinkle with the bacon. *Serves 12*

Chicken Parmigiano

2¼ pounds boneless skinless chicken breasts
3 cups (12 ounces) finely shredded Parmesan cheese
6 ounces fresh mozzarella cheese
3 large tomatoes
2 tablespoons olive oil
2 garlic cloves, minced
½ cup chicken broth
1 teaspoon salt
½ teaspoon pepper
12 whole fresh basil leaves
2 tablespoons julienned fresh basil
16 ounces pasta, cooked al dente

Preheat the oven to 200 degrees. Cut the chicken into twelve 3-ounce portions; pound thin. Coat on both sides with the Parmesan cheese. Cut the mozzarella cheese into twelve thin slices. Core and blanch the tomatoes; cool slightly and remove the skins. Cut the tomatoes into wedges and discard the seeds.

Heat a large sauté pan and add the olive oil. Add the chicken and sauté for 2 minutes or until brown on both sides, reducing the heat if the chicken browns too quickly. Remove to an ovenproof pan and keep warm in the oven.

Add the garlic to the drippings in the sauté pan and sauté for 30 seconds. Add the tomatos and sauté for 2 to 3 minutes. Stir in the broth, salt and pepper. Return the chicken to the sauté pan and top each medallion with one slice of mozzarella cheese and one basil leaf. Sprinkle the julienned basil into the simmering sauce and heat, covered, for 1 minute to melt the cheese.

Remove the chicken medallions to serving plates. Add the pasta to the sauce in the sauté pan and toss to coat evenly. Serve with the chicken. *Serves 6*

This is a light twist on an Italian classic.

Grilled Chicken Pasta with Vodka Sauce

1 1/4 pounds boneless skinless chicken breasts
Salt and pepper to taste
1 tablespoon olive oil
1 cup julienned onion
1/2 cup julienned red bell pepper
1 teaspoon minced garlic
1 cup vodka
1 1/2 cups Alfredo Sauce (page 54)
1 1/2 cups marinara sauce
16 ounces pasta, cooked al dente
1 cup (4 ounces) shredded Parmesan cheese

    Preheat the grill. Season the chicken with salt and pepper and place on the grill. Grill until cooked through. Cool slightly and cut into cubes.
    Heat a large skillet and add the olive oil. Add the onion and bell pepper and sauté for 4 minutes. Add the garlic and sauté for 1 minute longer. Remove form the heat and stir in the vodka. Return to the heat and ignite carefully. Allow the flames to die down and cook until reduced by one-half.
    Stir in the Alfredo Sauce and marinara sauce. Simmer for 4 minutes. Add the chicken and pasta and toss to coat evenly. Spoon onto plates or into pasta bowls; top with the cheese. *Serves 6*

This is an easy homemade version of a restaurant favorite. It is even easier if you make it with commercial Alfredo sauce and marinara sauce.

Sautéed Marinated Duck Breasts with Orange Brandy Demi-Glace

Sautéed Marinated Duck Breasts
1 cup brandy
1 cup red wine
1 cup orange-flavored extra-virgin olive oil
1 cup water
1/4 cup minced fresh thyme
1/4 cup minced fresh marjoram
1/4 cup salt
2 tablespoons cracked peppercorns
12 (6-ounce) skin-on duck breasts
2 tablespoons vegetable oil
1/2 cup brandy
1/2 cup orange juice

Orange Brandy Demi-Glace
1/2 cup minced shallots
2 tablespoons orange-flavored extra-virgin olive oil
1 cup brandy
2 cups orange juice
1 quart (4 cups) Demi-Glace (page 59)
Orange sections and fresh thyme, for garnish

Duck: Combine 1 cup brandy with the wine, olive oil, water, thyme, marjoram, salt and peppercorns in a bowl; mix well. Trim the excess fat from the duck and score the skin in a crisscross pattern. Add to the marinade, coating well. Marinate in the refrigerator overnight; drain.

Heat the vegetable oil in a large sauté pan. Add the duck skin side down and sear for 10 to 12 minutes. Turn the duck and sear for 5 to 6 minutes longer or until heated to 150 degrees internally. Remove the duck to a plate; slice the duck and keep warm.

Discard any excess oil or overbrowned bits from the sauté pan. Add 1/2 cup brandy and stir to deglaze the pan. Add the orange juice and cook until reduced by one-half. Reserve the reduction for the sauce.

Demi-Glace: Sauté the shallots in the olive oil in a sauté pan. Add the brandy and stir to deglaze the pan. Add the orange juice and cook until reduced by one-half. Stir in the Demi-Glace. Bring to a simmer and hold at 135 degrees. Stir in the reserved reduction. Spoon onto the serving plates and arrange the duck in the sauce. Garnish with orange sections and fresh thyme. *Serves 12*

Teriyaki-Seared Sirloin

6 (6-ounce) sirloin steaks
1 tablespoon Asian sesame-ginger seasoning
2 tablespoons canola oil
1/2 teaspoon minced garlic
2 tablespoons sake
2 tablespoons teriyaki basting sauce and glaze
2 tablespoons chopped scallions

Coat the steaks with sesame-ginger seasoning. Heat the canola oil to the smoking point in a large skillet. Add the steaks and sear for 3 minutes on each side for medium-rare. Remove the steaks to a plate.

Add the garlic and sake to the skillet. Stir in the teriyaki basting sauce and return the steaks to the skillet, turning to coat evenly. Let stand off the heat for 7 minutes. Cut into thin strips to serve. Top with the scallions. *Serve 6*

Veal Marsala

18 (2-ounce) top round veal medallions
2 cups all-purpose flour
1 tablespoon salt
1 teaspoon pepper
2 tablespoons clarified butter
1 cup sliced large white mushrooms
2 tablespoons minced shallots
1/2 teaspoon minced garlic
1 cup marsala
2 cups Demi-Glace (page 59) or brown sauce
1/2 cup heavy cream
1 tablespoon chopped fresh parsley

Pound the veal medallions 1/8 inch thick. Mix the flour, salt and pepper together. Coat the medallions in the flour mixture. Heat the clarified butter in a sauté pan until nearly smoking. Add the veal medallions in batches and sauté for about 45 seconds on each side. Remove the veal to a warm plate.

Scrape up and discard any overbrowned bits from the sauté pan. Add the mushrooms, shallots and garlic to the pan and sauté for 1 to 2 minutes. Add the wine and stir to deglaze the pan. Cook until the wine is reduced by one-half. Stir in the Demi-Glace and cream. Return the veal to the pan and simmer until the sauce is smooth, stirring frequently. Stir in the parsley. Place three veal medallions on each serving plate and spoon the sauce over the top. *Serves 6*

Grilled Lamb with Hazelnut Sauce

Hazelnut Sauce
3 slices fine-textured whole wheat bread
1/2 cup beef broth
1/4 cup apple juice
1 cup roasted hazelnuts
2 tablespoons white wine vinegar
1 tablespoon minced fresh garlic
2 teaspoons olive oil
Dash of ground red pepper
2 tablespoons chopped fresh parsley

Grilled Lamb
2 pounds lamb sirloin steaks or chops (3/4 inch thick)
1/2 teaspoon salt
1/2 teaspoon pepper
Chopped hazelnuts, for garnish

Sauce: Tear the bread into small cubes. Combine with the broth and apple juice in a small bowl. Let stand for 5 minutes. Process the hazelnuts in a food processor or blender until ground. Add the bread mixture, vinegar, garlic, olive oil and red pepper; process until smooth. Spoon into a bowl and chill in the refrigerator for several hours. Bring to room temperature and stir in the parsley at serving time.

Lamb: Preheat the grill or broiler. Season the lamb with the salt and pepper. Grill or broil four inches from the heat source for 3 to 5 minutes or until seared. Turn the lamb and grill or broil for 3 to 5 minutes longer or until done to taste. Serve with the sauce. Garnish with chopped hazelnuts. *Serves 4*

Pecan-Crusted Pork Loin with Sweet Potato Mash and Maple Hoisin Sauce

Sweet Potato Mash
3 cups mashed cooked sweet potatoes
1 tablespoon butter
1 tablespoon maple syrup
1 tablespoon brown sugar
1/2 teaspoon ground ginger
1/2 teaspoon ground allspice
Salt to taste

Pecan-Crusted Pork
2 1/4 pounds boneless pork loin
1 teaspoon salt
1/2 teaspoon pepper
1 cup pecans
1 cup panko (Japanese bread crumbs)
1/4 cup (or more) canola oil
1 tablespoon sesame oil
1 tablespoon minced shallot
1 teaspoon grated fresh ginger
2 tablespoons teriyaki basting sauce and glaze
2 tablespoons maple syrup
1 tablespoon hoisin sauce
Toasted pecans, for garnish

Mash: Combine the sweet potatoes with the butter, maple syrup, brown sugar, ginger, allspice and salt in a mixing bowl. Mix with a paddle attachment until smooth. Keep warm.

Pork: Cut the pork into twelve medallions 1/4 inch thick. Pound the pork medallions slightly and season with the salt and pepper. Pulse the pecans in a food processor until coarsely ground; mix with the bread crumbs in a bowl. Coat the pork medallions with the pecan mixture, pressing the coating firmly onto the surface.

Heat the canola oil in a large skillet. Add the pork in batches and sauté until golden brown on both sides, adding additional canola oil as needed. Remove the pork to a warm plate. Wipe out the sauté pan and add the sesame oil; heat slightly. Add the shallot and ginger and sauté lightly until the shallots are tender. Stir in the teriyaki basting sauce, maple syrup and hoisin sauce. Add the pork and cook until heated through, stirring to coat evenly.

Spoon or pipe the sweet potatoes onto serving plates and arrange the pork around the sweet potatoes. Garnish with toasted pecans. *Serves 6*

Enjoy the contemporary twist to these seasonal flavors.

Chef Pam's Chipotle-Crusted Pork Tenderloin

4 slices applewood-smoked bacon
1 (1- to 1 1/2-pound) pork tenderloin
1 cup Chef Pam's Collard Greens (page 81)
1 cup (4 ounces) shredded smoked Gouda cheese
1 cup Chipotle Dry Rub (page 63)

Preheat the oven to 400 degrees. Arrange the bacon on a baking sheet and bake for 15 to 20 minutes or until brown on top. Reduce the oven temperature to 350 degrees.

Butterfly the pork lengthwise and open flat on a work surface. Cover with plastic wrap and pound to an even thickness of 1/4 inch. Remove the plastic wrap. Spread the Collard Greens over the pork and top with the cheese. Roll from the long side to enclose the filling.

Roll in the Chipotle Dry Rub, coating evenly. Wrap with the bacon, placing the browned side down; secure with wooden picks. Place on a rack in a baking pan. Bake for 15 to 25 minutes or to 145 degrees internally. Let rest for 5 to 10 minutes before slicing. *Serves 4*

Pam Browning

Pork Tenderloin Amandine

2 1/2 pounds pork tenderloin, trimmed
Salt and pepper to taste
1/4 cup all-purpose flour
2 tablespoons clarified butter
2 shallots, minced
1/2 cup sliced blanched almonds
1/2 cup dry sherry
1 cup brown sauce or gravy
1/4 cup cream

Cut the pork into 2-ounce medallions and then pound 1/4 to 3/8 inch thick. Season with salt and pepper and coat with the flour. Heat a sauté pan over high heat and add 1 tablespoon of the clarified butter. Add the pork in batches, sautéing for 1 minute on each side; remove to a plate.

Scrape up and discard any overbrowned bits from the sauté pan. Add the remaining 1 tablespoon clarified butter and reduce the heat. Add the shallots and almonds and sauté just until the almonds begin to brown. Add the sherry, stirring to deglaze the skillet. Cook until reduced by one-half.

Stir in the brown sauce and cream and adjust the seasoning. Return the pork and any accumulated juices to the sauté pan. Simmer for 2 to 4 minutes or until slightly thickened. Place three medallions on each plate and spoon the sauce over the top. *Serves 6*

Southwestern Pork Medallions

2 tablespoons olive oil
3 pounds pork tenderloin or pork loin
1 tablespoon chili powder
1 teaspoon salt
1/4 cup diced onion
1 tablespoon minced garlic
2 hot chiles, diced
1 cup canned diced tomatoes
Hot cooked rice

   Preheat the grill. Rub the grill rack with a paper towel dipped in a small amount of the olive oil. Cut the pork into 2-ounce medallions; pound slightly. Coat the medallions with the chili powder and salt. Place on the grill and grill for 1 to 2 minutes on each side; remove and keep warm.
   Heat the remaining olive oil in a saucepan. Add the onion, garlic and chiles. Sauté until the onion is tender-crisp. Stir in the tomatoes. Simmer until the sauce is slightly thickened.
   Spoon rice onto serving plates. Top with the pork. Adjust the seasonings in the sauce and spoon over and around the pork. *Serves 6*

Rollatini Con Brisco

8 ounces thinly sliced pancetta
8 ounces thinly sliced prosciutto
1 (4-pound) center-cut pork loin
2 teaspoons kosher salt
2 teaspoons freshly ground pepper
2 cups (8 ounces) shredded Parmesan cheese
2 cups (8 ounces) shredded mozzarella cheese
2 tablespoons chopped fresh sage
2 cups all-purpose flour
4 eggs
1 cup water
1/2 cup seasoned bread crumbs
1 cup (4 ounces) grated Parmesan cheese
1 cup vegetable oil

Preheat the oven to 300 degrees. Place the pancetta and prosciutto on a baking pan. Bake until nearly crisp.

Trim any silver skin from the pork. Butterfly the pork horizontally and lay flat on a work surface. Continue to butterfly each side again until the pork measures about 12 inches by 12 inches. Cover with plastic wrap and pound until less than 1/2 inch thick, taking care to not tear any holes. Remove the plastic wrap. Season with the kosher salt and pepper.

Sprinkle the pork with 2 cups shredded Parmesan cheese, the mozzarella cheese and the sage; arrange the pancetta and prosciutto over the top. Roll the pork tightly to enclose the filling, securing with kitchen twine, if desired.

Arrange three large pans for a breading station. Fill one pan with the flour, one with a mixture of the eggs and water and one with a mixture of the bread crumbs and 1 cup grated Parmesan cheese. Coat the pork roll with the flour, dip into the egg wash and then coat with the bread crumb mixture; take care to keep the roll intact and to coat the ends.

Heat the oil in a large sauté pan. Sauté the roll until brown on all sides. Place on a baking sheet. Roast for about 1 hour or to 145 degrees internally. Let rest for 15 minutes before slicing. Serve with additional chopped sage and a brandy demi-glace. *Serves 10*

Hazelnut-Seared Catfish with Chive Beurre Blanc

Chive Beurre Blanc
1/2 cup dry white wine
1/4 cup white wine vinegar
1/4 cup finely minced shallots
1 cup (2 sticks) butter,
    cut into small pieces
2 tablespoons finely chopped chives
Salt and pepper to taste

Hazelnut-Seared Catfish
2 1/4 pounds catfish fillets
Salt and pepper to taste
1 cup finely minced hazelnuts
1/2 cup all-purpose flour
1/2 cup clarified butter

Sauce: Combine the wine, vinegar and shallots in a small saucepan and cook until reduced to 1/4 cup; remove from the heat. Add the butter gradually, stirring until well incorporated after each addition; the sauce should thicken as the butter is added. Add additional butter if necessary. Stir in the chives and season with salt and pepper. Hold at room temperature.

Catfish: Season the catfish fillets with salt and pepper. Mix the hazelnuts and flour. Press the catfish firmly into the hazelnut mixture, coating evenly on both sides.

Heat 1/4 cup of the clarified butter in a cast-iron skillet. Add half the fillets and sauté until golden brown on both sides and cooked through. Repeat with the remaining clarified butter and catfish. Spoon the Chive Beurre Blanc over the fish to serve. *Serves 6*

This was served at the Savoring Flavors Event.

Baked Halibut with Spinach, Feta and Pignoli

6 (6-ounce) halibut steaks
1 sprig of fresh oregano, finely chopped
1 sprig of fresh thyme, finely chopped
Kosher salt and freshly ground pepper to taste
4 cups packed baby spinach leaves
1 tablespoon minced shallot
1 teaspoon minced garlic
3 tablespoons extra-virgin olive oil
6 ounces crumbled feta cheese
2 tablespoons toasted pignoli (pine nuts)
2 tablespoons white wine
Olive oil
2 tablespoons fresh lemon juice

Preheat the oven to 400 degrees. Place the halibut steaks on a cutting board. Cut a horizontal pocket in each steak, cutting from one side to within 1/2 inch of the other. Season with the oregano, thyme, kosher salt and pepper.

Sauté the spinach with the shallot and garlic in 3 tablespoons olive oil in a sauté pan until wilted. Drain well and stir in the cheese and pignoli. Season with kosher salt and pepper. Sauté just until the cheese begins to bind the mixture.

Spoon the spinach mixture evenly into the pockets in the fish. Place in a baking dish and brush lightly with the wine and additional olive oil. Sprinkle with the lemon juice. Bake for 12 to 15 minutes or until the fish begins to brown and flakes easily. *Serves 6*

Enjoy a Mediterranean twist to this versatile fish.

Blackened Red Snapper with Cajun Hollandaise Sauce

6 (6-ounce) red snapper fillets or drum fillets
2 tablespoons clarified butter, melted
2 cups Cajun seasoning
1/4 cup clarified butter
2 cups Cajun Hollandaise Sauce (page 57)

Brush the fish fillets lightly with 2 tablespoons melted clarified butter. Coat with the Cajun seasoning, shaking off any excess. Heat 1/4 cup clarified butter in a large cast-iron skillet or heavy sauté pan. Add the fish and sauté for 3 minutes on each side or until deep russet brown; do not char or overbrown. Test to see if the fish flakes easily, finishing thicker fillets in the oven if necessary. Serve with the Cajun Hollandaise Sauce. *Serves 6*

Otto Steele
O'so Eats Restaurant

I first met Otto at Cherry Street Prison in Winston-Salem. I had been going in there as a volunteer for about two years, and one day came straight from work in my chef whites. Otto was drawn to me like a moth to a bug zapper.

"Are you a real chef?" he asked. Over the course of our conversation, Otto's passion for food became evident, and he let me know that during his incarceration he had completed a culinary training rotation via AB Tech in Asheville, North Carolina, and that he was eager for more training. I told him about TCK and encouraged him to enroll in our program, but was skeptical that he would actually follow through upon release. Nine months later Otto showed up in my classroom, fully enrolled and ready to go.

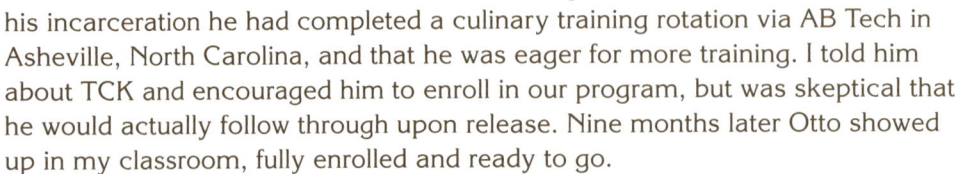

His passion and determination never flagged during his time at TCK. Otto graduated in July 2009 and was voted Most Valuable Classmate by his peers. Shortly after graduation we referred Otto to an opening at a new restaurant that had opened in Winston-Salem, O'so Eats, owned and headed by Sammy Gianopoulos, a local restaurateur from High Point.

Otto felt at home there right away. He has worked hard to get used to the fast-paced routines of a busy restaurant, but Sammy points out that Otto's great attitude earns him some extra time to learn the ropes. They are now in the process of training him for one of the more demanding line cook positions at the restaurant.

After Otto allowed drugs and alcohol to wreck his life and earn him seven years with the NC Department of Corrections, he is now focused on gaining back a normal life. "I just want to be a productive member of society," he says. "The relationships I damaged with my family are all coming back to me. Ultimately I want to go back into prison and give back to others what was so freely given to me."

Pesto Salmon

Pesto
1 cup fresh basil leaves, trimmed
1 bunch fresh parsley, trimmed
1/4 cup toasted pine nuts
1/4 cup garlic cloves
1 1/2 cups extra-virgin olive oil
1/4 cup (1 ounce) grated Parmesan cheese
Salt and freshly ground pepper to taste

Salmon
4 (8-ounce) salmon fillets
2 cups fresh spinach
1/4 cup (1/2 stick) butter
1 cup heavy cream
12 ounces whole wheat linguini
1/4 cup chopped sun-dried tomatoes

Pesto: Combine the basil, parsley and pine nuts in the food processor and pulse to chop coarsely. Add the garlic and pulse several times. Add the olive oil gradually, processing constantly until smooth, stopping to scrape down the side of the food processor with a rubber spatula. Add the cheese and pulse to mix well. Season with salt and pepper and spoon into a bowl.

Salmon: Spread 1/4 cup of the pesto over the salmon. Marinate in the refrigerator for 4 hours.

Preheat the oven to 375 degrees. Place the salmon on a baking sheet and bake for 10 to 20 minutes or until it flakes easily.

Cook the pasta using the package directions.

Sauté the spinach in the butter in a saucepan until wilted. Stir in the cream. Cook until reduced by one-half. Stir in 1 tablespoon of the pesto. Add the pasta and toss to coat evenly. Stir in the sun-dried tomatoes.

Spoon the pasta onto serving plates and top with the salmon. Store the remaining pesto in an airtight container in the refrigerator for another use.
Serves 4

Sammy Gianopoulos and Otto Steele, O'so Eats Restaurant

Pecan-Crusted Mountain Trout with Sage Browned Butter

Sage Browned Butter
3/4 cup (1 1/2 sticks) butter
4 ounces fresh sage, julienned

Pecan-Crusted Mountain Trout
4 cups pecans
4 pounds mountain trout fillets or other
   cold-water trout fillets
Salt and pepper to taste
1 cup clarified butter
1 lemon, thinly sliced, for garnish
2 tablespoons chopped fresh parsley, for garnish

   Butter: Heat the butter in a sauté pan until it begins to foam. Add the sage and reduce the heat to very low. Cook until the butter is light brown and the sage is toasted. Remove from the heat.
   Trout: Preheat the oven to 400 degrees. Pulse the pecans in a food processor until finely ground. Spoon into a large shallow pan. Season the trout with salt and pepper. Press cut side down firmly into the pecans to coat evenly.
   Heat the clarified butter in a large sauté pan and add the trout skin side up. Sauté until seared and brown. Remove from the sauté pan and place skin side down on a baking sheet. Bake for 5 minutes or until cooked through. Place on serving plates and drizzle with the Sage Browned Butter. Garnish with lemon slices and parsley. *Serves 6*

Chile-Rubbed Tuna with Mango Salsa

Mango Salsa
1/2 mango, diced
2 scallions, diced
1 tomato, diced
1/4 cup chopped cilantro
2 teaspoons minced garlic
2 tablespoons honey
2 tablespoons fresh lime juice
1 tablespoon chili powder
1 teaspoon salt

Chile-Rubbed Tuna
1 serrano chile, seeded and chopped
1 canned chipotle chile in adobo sauce
1 jalapeño chile, seeded and chopped
1 tablespoon honey
1 tablespoon paprika
1 tablespoon fresh lime juice
1 teaspoon grated lime zest
2 teaspoons ground cumin
2 teaspoons kosher salt
6 (6-ounce) tuna steaks

Salsa: Combine the mango, scallions, tomato, cilantro and garlic in a bowl. Stir in the honey, lime juice, chili powder and salt. Store in the refrigerator for 2 hours or longer before serving. Serve chilled or at room temperature.

Tuna: Combine the serrano chile, chipotle chile and jalapeño chile in a food processor. Add the honey, paprika, lime juice, lime zest, cumin and kosher salt; process at high speed until puréed. Combine with the tuna in a bowl, turning to coat evenly. Marinate in the refrigerator for 2 to 4 hours.

Preheat the grill. Grill the tuna for 3 to 4 minutes. Turn the tuna and brush with the marinade. Grill for 3 to 4 minutes longer or until the fish flakes easily. Serve with the salsa for a southwestern seafood specialty dish. *Serves 6*

Butter-Poached Lobster

2 pounds lobster tail meat, one shell reserved
1 1/4 cups (2 1/2 sticks) butter
2 tablespoons fresh lime juice
2 tablespoons fresh lemon juice
1 teaspoon grated lime zest
1 teaspoon grated lemon zest
1 teaspoon minced fresh basil
1 teaspoon minced fresh rosemary
1 teaspoon minced fresh thyme
1 teaspoon minced fresh marjoram
1 fresh bay leaf
Salt to taste
Hot cooked rice, risotto or pasta

   Melt the butter in a saucepan and heat to 165 to 180 degrees; the temperature of the butter is essential for poaching the lobster. Add the lime juice, lemon juice, lime zest, lemon zest, basil, rosemary, thyme, marjoram, bay leaf and salt; mix well. Add the lobster and reserved shell to the butter; the lobster should be covered by the butter. Poach for 4 minutes or just until the lobster is cooked. Remove the lobster from the poaching liquid and slice into medallions. Serve over rice, risotto or pasta. *Serves 6*

You can discard the lobster shell and bay leaf and use the reserved poaching butter for a pasta sauce, if desired.

Ginger-Seared Scallops with Blood Orange Sauce

18 (10-count) sea scallops (about 2 pounds)
1 teaspoon ginger
1 1/2 teaspoons kosher salt
1/2 teaspoon freshly ground pepper
6 tablespoons cornstarch
2 tablespoons canola oil
Blood Orange Sauce (page 56)
1 teaspoon grated orange zest, for garnish
1 teaspoon chopped fresh mint, for garnish

Pat the scallops dry. Mix the ginger, kosher salt and pepper together. Season the scallops with the seasoning mixture and coat the top and bottom lightly with the cornstarch. Heat the canola oil in a sauté pan until very hot. Add the scallops and sear for 1 1/2 to 2 minutes on each side; drain on paper towels. Serve with Blood Orange Sauce and garnish with the orange zest and mint. *Serves 6*

Sautéed Shrimp Scampi

1 pound medium shrimp, peeled and deveined
3/4 cup (1 1/2 sticks) butter
1 tablespoon minced garlic
1/2 cup white wine
1/2 cup chicken broth
1/4 cup fresh lemon juice
2 tablespoons chopped scallions
1 tablespoon finely chopped fresh parsley
1/2 teaspoon salt
1/2 teaspoon coarsely ground pepper
4 cups cooked pasta
3 tablespoons grated Parmesan cheese

Sauté the shrimp in 2 tablespoons of the butter until partially cooked. Add the garlic and sauté for 30 seconds. Stir in the wine, broth and lemon juice. Simmer until reduced by one-half. Add the scallions, parsley, salt and pepper. Reduce the heat to very low and stir in the remaining butter gradually, cooking until the sauce is thickened and smooth. Toss with the pasta in a bowl. Spoon onto serving plates and top with the cheese. *Serves 6*

Rustic Tuscan Pasta with Shrimp and Sausage

2 cups uncooked ziti or other hearty pasta
Olive oil
1 pound Italian sausage links
1 teaspoon paprika
1 teaspoon garlic powder
1/2 teaspoon salt
1/2 teaspoon pepper
1 pound (21- to 25-count) shrimp, peeled and deveined
2 tablespoons olive oil
3 scallion bulbs, chopped
1/2 cup finely diced Anaheim chiles
1 1/2 pounds Roma tomatoes, cut into halves and sliced
1 cup white wine
6 garlic cloves, minced
1/4 cup chopped fresh basil
2 tablespoons chopped fresh oregano
2 tablespoons chopped fresh parsley
Stems of 3 scallions, chopped
1/4 teaspoon crushed red pepper flakes
2 tablespoons butter
Grated Parmesan cheese, for garnish

Cook the pasta using the package directions; drain. Drizzle with a small amount of olive oil and keep warm. Cut the sausage into 1/2-inch slices. Sauté in a nonstick skillet until brown; keep warm.

Mix the paprika, garlic powder, salt and pepper together. Rub generously over the shrimp. Heat a sauté pan and add 2 tablespoons olive oil. Add the shrimp and sauté for 3 minutes. Add the scallion bulbs, Anaheim chiles, tomatoes, wine and garlic. Sauté until the liquid has nearly evaporated. Stir in the basil, oregano, parsley, scallion stems, crushed red pepper, sausage and pasta; toss to mix well. Cook until heated through. Add the butter and spoon onto serving plates. Garnish with Parmesan cheese. *Serves 6*

Vanilla-Scented Baby Vegetables

18 baby carrots with tops
18 baby patty pan squash or baby yellow squash
18 baby zucchini
1 tablespoon clarified butter
1/4 teaspoon vanilla bean seeds
Salt and pepper to taste

Peel the carrots and cut the stems short. Blanch the carrots, patty pan squash and zucchini in boiling water in a saucepan for 5 minutes or until tender-crisp; drain. Heat the clarified butter in a sauté pan and add the vegetables, vanilla bean seeds, salt and pepper. Sauté just until well seasoned. *Serves 6*

Island Vegetable Medley

5 shallots, cut into halves
2 chayotes, peeled and coarsely diced
1 large carrot, cut horizontally and sliced
1 small butternut squash, peeled and coarsely diced
1/2 cup coarsely diced red bell pepper
1/4 cup olive oil
3 tablespoons dried thyme
2 teaspoons coarse salt
2 teaspoons black pepper
1/2 pineapple
1/2 cup finely diced red onion
1 1/2 tablespoons minced garlic
Olive oil
1 cup chopped fresh kale
1/2 cup chicken stock
Salt and pepper to taste

Preheat the oven to 400 degrees. Mix the shallots, chayotes, carrot, butternut squash and bell pepper in a bowl. Add 1/4 cup olive oil, the thyme, 2 teaspoons coarse salt and 2 teaspoons pepper; toss to coat evenly. Spread on a baking sheet and roast for 25 minutes or until the vegetables are tender and golden brown.

Preheat the grill. Cut the pineapple into quarters and grill for 5 to 7 minutes on each side or until marked with the grill but not overbrowned. Cut into large dice.

Sauté the onion and garlic in a small amount of olive oil in a sauté pan until translucent. Add the kale and stock; season with salt and pepper to taste. Cook until the kale is tender. Add the pineapple and the roasted vegetables. Cook until heated through. *Serves 8*

Pam Browning

Whipped Sweet Potatoes with Roasted Granny Smith Apples

3 sweet potatoes
2 Granny Smith apples, peeled, cored and diced
3 tablespoons olive oil
1 tablespoon dried thyme
1 teaspoon coarse salt
1 teaspoon black pepper
1/2 cup heavy cream
1/2 cup (1 stick) butter
1/2 teaspoon cinnamon
Salt and pepper to taste

Preheat the oven to 400 degrees. Place the sweet potatoes on a baking sheet and bake for 1 hour or until tender. Peel and chop the sweet potatoes. Mix the apples with the olive oil, thyme, coarse salt and 1 teaspoon pepper in a bowl. Spread on a baking sheet. Roast for 15 minutes or until tender and golden brown. Combine the sweet potatoes and apple mixture in a mixing bowl and beat until well mixed.

Heat the cream with the butter in a saucepan. Add to the sweet potatoes. Add the cinnamon and salt and pepper to taste. Beat until smooth. *Serves 6*

Pam Browning

Sweets

Triad Community Kitchen

Jerome Timberlake
Independence Village Retirement Community

Jerome Timberlake was a member of the first class ever offered at the Triad Community Kitchen, the Alpha Class. Numbering only eleven students to start, things were a lot different then. (We now regularly max out with twenty or even more students enrolled.)

Jerome and his classmates were trailblazers of sorts. We had never tried out our curriculum on live humans before; we didn't really know how well this concept would work. The idea of putting all of these folk from wildly diverse backgrounds into one pressure-packed, hot, intense culinary environment had more than a few folk slightly worried. Jerome was not worried, however. He was ready and determined to learn. He had made a couple of attempts at more conventional culinary schools but just was unable to afford the expense, especially while trying to maintain employment.

Jerome had had enough of dead-end jobs and was ready to do whatever it took to begin a career in culinary arts. He worked a third shift job his entire semester at TCK and would often rush into class straight from work early in the morning. Upon graduation Jerome secured employment as a cook at Old Vineyard Behavioral Health, where he gained experience for almost two years. He then did a subsequent stint at the JH Adams Inn for another nine months. Jerome was hired as the Assistant Director of Food Service at Independence Village in 2010.

Jerome says of his success, "I am persistent and don't give up. I'm willing to do what it takes to achieve goals. I want to become a great chef, so I won't give up until I achieve it."

Seven-Flavor Pound Cake

Cake
3 cups all-purpose flour
1/2 teaspoon baking powder
1 cup milk
1 teaspoon coconut extract
1 teaspoon lemon extract
1 teaspoon rum extract
1 teaspoon butter extract
1 teaspoon vanilla extract
4 drops of pineapple oil
4 drops of cherry oil
1 cup (2 sticks) butter, softened
1/2 cup shortening
3 cups sugar
5 eggs, beaten individually

Seven-Flavor Glaze
1/2 cup sugar
1/4 cup water
1 teaspoon coconut extract
1 teaspoon lemon extract
1 teaspoon rum extract
1 teaspoon butter extract
1 teaspoon vanilla extract
4 drops of pineapple oil
4 drops of cherry oil

Cake: Preheat the oven to 325 degrees. Mix the flour and baking powder together. Blend the milk with the coconut extract, lemon extract, rum extract, butter extract, vanilla extract, pineapple oil and cherry oil in a small bowl.

Cream the butter, shortening and sugar in a large mixing bowl until light and fluffy. Add the eggs one at a time, mixing well after each addition. Add the flour mixture gradually, mixing well. Mix in the milk mixture. Spoon into a sprayed and floured bundt pan. Bake for 1 1/2 hours. Cool in the pan for 10 minutes; remove to a serving plate.

Glaze: Combine the sugar, water, coconut extract, lemon extract, rum extract, butter extract, vanilla extract, pineapple oil and cherry oil in a saucepan. Cook until the sugar melts and the glaze thickens, stirring constantly. Drizzle or brush over the cake. *Serves 14*

Jerome Timberlake, Independence Village Retirement Community

Cinnamon Wine Cake

Cake
1 (2-layer) package yellow cake mix
1 (3-ounce) package vanilla instant pudding mix
1/4 cup granulated sugar
1/4 cup packed brown sugar
2 teaspoons cinnamon
4 eggs
3/4 cup vegetable oil
3/4 cup water
1/4 cup brandy
1/4 cup white wine

Brandy Wine Glaze
1/2 cup (1 stick) butter
1/2 cup sugar
1/4 cup brandy
1/4 cup white wine

Cake: Preheat the oven to 325 degrees. Mix the cake mix, pudding mix, granulated sugar, brown sugar and cinnamon in a bowl. Add the eggs, oil, water, brandy and wine; stir to mix well. Spoon into a buttered and floured bundt pan. Bake for 1 hour. Cool in the pan on a rack. Pierce multiple times with a wooden pick.

Glaze: Melt the butter in a small saucepan. Stir in the sugar, brandy and wine. Bring to a boil and boil for at least 1 minute, stirring constantly. Spoon over the cake in the pan and let stand for 1 hour before removing to a serving plate. *Serves 14*

William Webster

Kentucky Butter Rum Cake

Cake
3 cups unsifted all-purpose flour
1 teaspoon baking powder
1/2 teaspoon baking soda
1 teaspoon salt
1 cup buttermilk or sour milk
2 teaspoons vanilla extract
1 cup (2 sticks) butter or margarine, softened
1 3/4 cups sugar
4 eggs

Butter Rum Sauce
3/4 cup sugar
1/4 cup water
1/2 cup (1 stick) butter
1 tablespoon rum extract

Cake: Preheat the oven to 325 degrees. Mix the flour, baking powder, baking soda and salt together. Blend the buttermilk and vanilla in a cup.

Cream the butter in a large mixing bowl until smooth. Add the sugar and beat until light and fluffy. Beat in the eggs one at a time. Add the dry ingredients alternately with the buttermilk mixture, mixing at low speed after each addition. Beat at medium speed for 2 minutes, scraping the bowl occasionally.

Spoon into a greased 10-inch bundt pan or tube pan. Bake for 60 to 65 minutes or until a tester comes out clean. Pierce the cake with a long-tined fork.

Sauce: Combine the sugar, water and butter in a saucepan. Cook until the butter is melted; do not allow to boil. Remove from the heat and stir in the rum extract. Pour over the warm cake in the pan. When the cake is completely cool, you can invert it onto a serving plate. Sprinkle with confectioner's sugar at serving time, if desired. *Serves 14*

If you do not have buttermilk, you can add a small amount of vinegar to milk to sour it.

Deborah B. Lane

Rum Carrot Cake

Cake
2 cups self-rising flour
2 cups sugar
4 eggs
1 1/4 cups vegetable oil
2 (4-ounce) jars carrot baby food
1/4 cup minced carrots
1 tablespoon golden rum
2 teaspoons cinnamon

Rum Icing
1/2 cup (1 stick) butter, softened
2 tablespoons cream cheese, softened
2 cups confectioners' sugar
1 egg yolk
1 tablespoon golden rum

Cake: Preheat the oven to 325 degrees. Combine the flour, sugar, eggs, oil, baby food, carrots, rum and cinnamon in a mixing bowl and mix well. Spoon into two greased and floured 9-inch cake pans. Bake for 35 to 45 minutes or until a tester comes out clean. Cool in the pan for 10 minutes; remove to a wire rack to cool completely.

Icing: Beat the butter and cream cheese in a mixing bowl until light. Add the confectioners' sugar and beat until fluffy. Beat in the egg yolk and rum. Spread between the layers and over the top and side of the cake. *Serves 14*

If you are concerned about using a raw egg yolk, use an egg yolk from an egg that has been pasteurized in its shell, which is sold at some specialty food stores, or use an equivalent amount of pasteurized egg yolk substitute.

William Webster

Pink Lemonade Cake

Cake
1 (2-layer) package yellow cake mix
1 (3-ounce) package lemon pudding mix
1/4 cup sugar
4 eggs
3/4 cup vegetable oil
3/4 cup water
1/2 cup frozen pink lemonade concentrate, thawed

Lemonade Sauce
1/2 cup sugar
1/2 cup (1 stick) butter
1/2 cup frozen pink lemonade concentrate, thawed

Lemonade Glaze
1/2 cup confectioners' sugar
1 tablespoon (about) frozen pink lemonade concentrate, thawed

Cake: Preheat the oven to 325 degrees. Mix the cake mix, pudding mix and sugar in a large bowl. Add the eggs, oil, water and pink lemonade concentrate; beat just until smooth. Spoon into a buttered and floured bundt pan. Bake for 1 hour. Place in the pan on a wire rack.

Sauce: Combine the sugar, butter and pink lemonade concentrate in a small saucepan and bring to a boil. Spoon over the cake in the pan. Invert the cake on a serving plate when cool.

Glaze: Combine the confectioners' sugar and enough pink lemonade concentrate to make of drizzling consistency, mixing well. Drizzle over the cooled cake.

Serves 14

William Webster

Orange Cranberry Cake

Cake
1 (2-layer) package Duncan Hines® orange supreme cake mix
1 (3-ounce) package vanilla instant pudding mix
4 eggs
1 1/2 cups fresh orange juice
1 cup vegetable oil
3/4 cup dried cranberries
1/2 cup chopped pecans

Orange Cranberry Glaze
1 cup confectioners' sugar
2 teaspoons fresh orange juice
2 tablespoons dried cranberries
2 tablespoons chopped pecans
1 tablespoon grated orange zest

Cake: Preheat the oven to 350 degrees. Combine the cake mix, pudding mix, eggs, orange juice and oil in a mixing bowl and mix well. Fold in the dried cranberries and pecans. Spoon into a greased and floured bundt pan. Bake for 50 to 60 minutes or until a tester comes out clean. Cool in the pan for 15 minutes before inverting onto a serving plate.

Glaze: Combine the confectioners' sugar, orange juice, dried cranberries, pecans and orange zest in a mixing bowl; mix well. Spoon over the warm cake.
Serves 14

Pam Browning

Sweet Potato Cake

4 1/2 cups all-purpose flour, sifted
1 tablespoon baking powder
3/4 teaspoon baking soda
2 teaspoons cinnamon
Pinch of ground allspice
1/4 teaspoon salt
1 1/2 cups (3 sticks) butter, softened
3 cups firmly packed brown sugar
6 eggs
3 cups mashed canned sweet potatoes
3/4 cup milk
Maple Cream Cheese Frosting (page 126)

Preheat the oven to 350 degrees. Sift the flour, baking powder, baking soda, cinnamon, allspice and salt together.

Cream the butter and brown sugar in a mixing bowl until light and fluffy. Beat in the eggs one at a time. Add the sweet potatoes and mix well. Add the dry ingredients alternately with the milk, beginning and ending with the dry ingredients and mixing well after each addition.

Spoon into three greased 8-inch cake pans. Bake for 30 minutes or until the cake springs back when touched lightly with your finger. Cool in the pans for 10 minutes and then invert onto a serving plate to cool completely.

Spread Maple Cream Cheese Frosting between the layers and over the top and side of the cooled cake. *Serves 14*

You can also bake this in paper-lined muffin cups for 20 minutes and frost.

Maple Cream Cheese Frosting

1 1/2 cups (3 sticks) butter, softened
24 ounces cream cheese, softened
1/4 cup maple syrup
1/2 teaspoon cinnamon
8 cups confectioners' sugar

Cream the butter and cream cheese in the bowl of a standing mixer until light. Add the maple syrup and cinnamon and mix well. Beat in the confectioners' sugar gradually. *Makes 6 cups*

Basic Cheesecake

2 cups graham cracker crumbs
1/2 cup sugar
1/2 cup (1 stick) butter, melted
32 ounces cream cheese, softened
1 1/2 cups sugar

5 eggs
3 egg yolks
1/2 cup heavy cream
1/2 tablespoon vanilla extract

   Preheat the oven to 325 degrees. Mix the graham cracker crumbs, 1/2 cup sugar and the butter in a bowl. Press over the bottom of a buttered springform pan.
   Beat the cream cheese and 1 1/2 cups sugar in a mixing bowl until light and fluffy. Beat in the eggs, egg yolks, cream and vanilla. Spoon into the crust.
   Place the springform pan in a larger baking pan with enough water to reach halfway up the side of the springform pan. Bake for 1 to 1 1/2 hours or until the center is set. Cool to room temperature on a wire rack. Place on a serving plate and remove the side of the pan. Chill until serving time. *Serves 16*

Peppermint Cheesecake

2 cups Nabisco Famous Chocolate Wafer® cookie crumbs
1/4 cup (1/2 stick) butter, melted
1/2 cup peppermint candies
3/4 cup cream
24 ounces cream cheese, softened
1 1/4 cups sugar
1 teaspoon vanilla extract
1 teaspoon peppermint extract
2 eggs
6 egg yolks
2 drops of red food coloring
16 Nabisco Famous Chocolate Wafers® and 1 additional peppermint, for garnish

   Preheat the oven to 350 degrees. Mix the cookie crumbs and butter in a bowl. Press over the bottom and 1/2 inch up the side of a greased 9-inch springform pan.
   Crush the peppermints very fine or pulse in a food processor until very fine. Bring the cream to a simmer in a saucepan. Add half the crushed mints and cook until melted, stirring frequently.
   Beat the cream cheese and sugar in a large mixing bowl until light and fluffy. Add the vanilla extract and peppermint extract. Reserve 1 cup of the mixture for the topping. Beat the eggs and egg yolks into the remaining cream cheese mixture. Remove half the filling to a small bowl.
   Add the peppermint mixture to the filling in the large mixing bowl; mix well. Mix in the food coloring. Spoon the peppermint filling into the crust. Spoon the filling in the small bowl into the center of the peppermint filling. Swirl through the fillings with a table knife, swirling from the outer edge to the center; do not disturb the crust. Sprinkle with the remaining mints.
   Place the springform pan in a larger baking pan with enough water to reach halfway up the side of the springform pan. Bake for 1 to 1 1/2 hours or until the center is set. Cool to room temperature on a wire rack. Place on a serving plate and remove the side of the pan. Chill until serving time.
   Pipe the reserved 1 cup topping mixture into sixteen rosettes around the edge of the cheesecake and add one in the center. Garnish by standing one chocolate cookie in the center of each rosette around the edge and placing an additional mint on the center rosette. *Serves 16*

You can substitute Oreo® cookies for the Nabisco® cookies and omit the butter in the crust.

Carrot Cheesecake

3 cups pecan shortbread cookie crumbs
1/2 cup (1 stick) melted butter
1/2 cup sugar
24 ounces cream cheese, softened
1 cup sugar
1 1/2 cups puréed cooked carrots

3 egg yolks
5 eggs
1/2 teaspoon cinnamon
1/4 teaspoon allspice
Pinch of ground cloves
1/2 tablespoon vanilla extract

Preheat the oven to 325 degrees. Mix the cookie crumbs, butter and 1/2 cup sugar in a bowl. Press over the bottom of a greased springform pan.

Beat the cream cheese with 1 cup sugar in a mixing bowl until smooth. Beat in the carrots. Add the egg yolks, eggs, cinnamon, allspice, cloves and vanilla; mix well. Spoon into the crust.

Place the springform pan in a larger baking pan with enough water to reach halfway up the side of the springform pan. Bake for 1 to 1 1/2 hours or until the center is set. Cool to room temperature on a wire rack. Place on a serving plate and remove the side of the pan. Chill until serving time. *Serves 16*

For a seasonal variation, you can substitute a large can of pumpkin for the carrots.

Tiramisu Cheesecake

Cheesecake
2 cups finely ground shortbread
  cookie crumbs
1/2 cup (1 stick) butter, melted
3/4 cup heavy cream
1 cup chopped semisweet chocolate
20 ounces cream cheese, softened
3/4 cup sugar
3 egg yolks
4 eggs
2 teaspoons vanilla extract
7 tablespoons strong brewed
  espresso, cooled

Tiramisu Topping
4 ounces cream cheese, softened
1/4 cup sugar
1/2 teaspoon vanilla extract
1 tablespoon powdered
  hot chocolate mix
8 ounces cream cheese, softened
1/2 cup sugar
1 tablespoon strong brewed
  espresso, cooled

Cheesecake: Preheat the oven to 325 degrees. Mix the cookie crumbs with the butter in a bowl. Press over the bottom and three-fourths up the side of a 9-inch springform pan.

Heat the heavy cream in a small saucepan. Combine with the chocolate in a small bowl; stir until the chocolate melts and forms a smooth ganache. Reserve 2 tablespoons of the ganache for the topping.

Beat the cream cheese with the sugar in a mixing bowl until smooth. Beat in the egg yolks and eggs. Add 1/2 cup of the cream cheese mixture to the ganache in the small bowl; mix well. Divide the remaining cheesecake mixture into two portions. Stir the vanilla into one portion and the espresso into the other.

Spoon the ganache-flavored cheesecake mixture into the prepared crust, tilting to cover evenly. Spoon the vanilla-flavored cheesecake mixture evenly over the ganache. Spoon the espresso-flavored cheesecake mixture evenly over the vanilla mixture.

Place the springform pan in a larger baking pan with enough water to reach halfway up the side of the springform pan. Bake for 1 to 1 1/2 hours or until the center is set. Cool to room temperature on a wire rack. Place on a serving plate and remove the side of the pan.

Topping: Combine 4 ounces cream cheese with 1/4 cup sugar and the vanilla in a small mixing bowl and beat until smooth. Spread over the cheesecake. Dust with the hot chocolate mix, using a shaker or sifter.

Place the reserved 2 tablespoons ganache in a small plastic bag. Microwave for 5 seconds at a time until soft enough to pipe. Cut off a small corner of the bag and pipe in stripes across the cheesecake.

Combine 8 ounces cream cheese with 1/2 cup sugar and the espresso in a small mixing bowl and beat until smooth. Pipe rosettes around the edge of the cheesecake. Chill until serving time. *Serves 16*

Atchafalaya Bread Pudding with Caramel Rum Sauce

Pudding
12 large slices French bread
2 tablespoons butter, softened
1/2 cup dried currants or raisins
2 cups milk
1 cup heavy cream
1 cup sugar
4 egg yolks
3 eggs

1 tablespoon vanilla extract
1/4 teaspoon nutmeg
Pinch of salt

Caramel Rum Sauce
1 cup heavy cream
1 cup packed brown sugar
1/2 cup light corn syrup
1/4 cup dark rum

Pudding: Preheat the oven to 350 degrees. Spread one side of each bread slice with the butter. Arrange one layer of the bread buttered side up in a buttered baking pan. Sprinkle with the currants. Repeat the layers.

Combine the milk, cream, sugar, egg yolks, eggs, vanilla, nutmeg and salt in a large bowl. Whisk to mix well and strain. Spoon evenly over the bread layers. Let stand for 15 minutes. Bake for 45 minutes or until the center is set and the top is golden brown; if using a convection oven, set the fan at low speed.

Sauce: Combine the cream, brown sugar, corn syrup and rum in a saucepan. Bring to a boil over medium heat, stirring to mix well. Reduce the heat and simmer until the sauce is thick enough to coat a spoon. Serve with the bread pudding. *Serves 10*

You can make this in advance, store it in the refrigerator, and reheat to serve.

Paula's Sweet Potato Bread Pudding with Pecan Crumble

Pudding
2 cups milk
1 1/2 cups puréed Stokes County purple sweet potatoes
1/2 cup granulated sugar
1/2 cup packed brown sugar
1/2 teaspoon cinnamon
1/4 teaspoon nutmeg
2 teaspoons vanilla extract
6 egg yolks
2 eggs
2 loaves Italian bread, sliced 1 inch thick

Pecan Crumble
1 cup all-purpose flour
1 cup packed brown sugar
1/2 cup quick-cooking oats
1/2 cup toasted chopped pecans
1/2 cup (1 stick) chilled unsalted butter, diced

Pudding: Combine the milk, sweet potato purée, granulated sugar, brown sugar, cinnamon, nutmeg and vanilla in a medium saucepan; mix well. Bring just to a boil over medium-high heat. Remove from the heat. Whisk the egg yolks and eggs in a medium bowl until smooth. Ladle 1/2 cup of the hot milk mixture in a steady stream into the egg mixture, whisking constantly. Repeat the process. Add the egg mixture to the remaining hot milk. Cook over medium-high heat for 3 to 5 minutes or until thick enough to coat the back of a spoon, stirring constantly. Strain the mixture. Layer the bread and custard one-fourth at a time in a generously buttered 9×13-inch baking dish, beginning with the bread. Chill, covered, in the refrigerator overnight.

Crumble: Combine the flour, brown sugar, oats, pecans and butter in a bowl; mix until crumbly. Sprinkle over the pudding. To finish the pudding, preheat the oven to 350 degrees. Bake for 45 minutes or until the topping is golden brown and the pudding is bubbly. Serve warm. *Serves 10*

This variation on a Paula Deen classic works equally well with regular orange sweet potatoes. This version has received the "thumbs-up" from Paula herself. You can also serve it with Caramel Rum Sauce (page 131).

Classic Tarte Tatin

Tarte Crust
1 1/3 cups all-purpose flour
1/4 cup sugar
1/2 teaspoon salt
10 tablespoons unsalted butter, sliced 1/2 inch thick
6 tablespoons sour cream

Tarte
1/2 cup (1 stick) unsalted butter, softened
1 cup granulated sugar
1/4 cup packed light brown sugar
10 small Granny Smith apples, peeled, cored and cut into quarters
2 teaspoons lemon juice

Crust: Combine the flour, sugar and salt in a food processor and mix for 5 seconds. Add the butter and pulse to form coarse crumbs. Add 5 tablespoons of the sour cream and pulse until clumps begin to form; add the remaining 1 tablespoon sour cream if needed to bind.

Form the dough into a ball and flatten into a disk. Wrap in plastic wrap and chill for 2 to 24 hours. Roll into a 13-inch circle on a floured surface and slide onto a rimless baking sheet. Chill until ready to use.

Tarte: Preheat the oven 425 degrees. Heat a 12-inch ovenproof skillet and add the butter, granulated sugar and brown sugar; whisk to mix well. Remove from the heat and arrange the apple quarters cut side down around the outer edge of the skillet, crowding tightly. Add concentric circles until the bottom of the skillet is covered. Sprinkle with the lemon juice.

Cook over medium heat until a thick, deep amber syrup is formed, filling in any spaces that form with additional apples. Remove from the heat. Slide the chilled crust on top of the apples and press the edges down around the edge. Cut slits in the crust to vent.

Bake for 35 minutes or until the crust is deep golden brown. Cool for 5 minutes and then cut around the edge of the tarte to loosen it from the skillet. Place a large platter over the skillet and invert the tarte onto the platter; let stand for 3 minutes. Lift off the skillet gradually, rearranging any apples that slip out of place. Let stand for 30 minutes or longer. *Serves 10*

This classic, simple dish truly stands the test of time. The simple ingredients and methods let the apple flavor shine through.

Chocolate Caramel Macadamia Tart

Classic Tart Crust
1 cup all-purpose flour
1/3 cup confectioners' sugar
3/4 teaspoon salt
1/2 cup (1 stick) butter, sliced
 1/4 inch thick
1 tablespoon ice water

Tart
1/3 cup heavy cream
8 ounces bittersweet chocolate chips
1 1/2 cups macadamia nuts
1 1/4 cups sugar
1/3 cup water
1/2 cup heavy cream
1/4 cup (1/2 stick) butter
1 teaspoon vanilla extract
1/2 teaspoon salt

Crust: Whisk the flour, confectioners' sugar and salt together in a bowl. Add the butter and mix with a mixer or pastry blender or pulse in a food processor until the mixture forms coarse crumbs. Add the ice water gradually and mix to form a dough. Press into a tart pan with floured fingers. Chill for 1 hour.

Preheat the oven to 375 degrees. Place pie weights in the crust and bake for 16 minutes or until the edges begin to brown and the pastry is set. Remove the weights and bake for 10 to 12 minutes longer or until golden brown. Cool in the pan.

Tart: Bring 1/3 cup cream to a simmer in a heavy saucepan. Remove from the heat and add the chocolate chips, stirring to form a smooth ganache. Remove about one-tenth of the mixture to a small plastic bag and reserve.

Spread the remaining ganache in the prepared crust and sprinkle with the macadamia nuts. Place in the freezer while preparing the filling.

Combine the sugar and water in a large deep saucepan. Cook over medium-high heat until the sugar dissolves, stirring constantly. Increase the heat and boil, without stirring, until the syrup is golden brown. Add 1/2 cup cream and the butter carefully to avoid splatters, stirring until smooth. Boil without stirring until a candy thermometer reaches 240 degrees. Remove from the heat and whisk in the vanilla and salt.

Spoon the caramel into the crust; shake the tart pan gently to settle the filling. Cool at room temperature for 3 hours.

Microwave the reserved ganache on High for 6 seconds at a time until warm enough to pipe. Cut off a small corner of the bag and pipe a crisscross pattern over the filling. *Serves 12*

This recipe involves several steps, but the individual principles are easy to master. You can experiment by substituting walnuts or using a combination of nuts.

Sweet Potato Torte

Torte Crust
2 cups all-purpose flour
1 tablespoon sugar
3/4 teaspoon salt
3/4 cup shortening, chilled
2 tablespoons (or more) ice water
2 tablespoons vegetable oil
1 egg yolk
1 1/2 teaspoons white vinegar

Torte
2 1/4 pounds sweet potatoes
1 3/4 cups sweetened condensed milk
6 tablespoons unsalted butter, melted
2 eggs
1/4 cup honey
2 tablespoons maple syrup
3/4 teaspoon vanilla extract
1 teaspoon salt

Crust: Combine the flour, sugar and salt in a food processor and process for 10 seconds. Add the shortening and pulse until the mixture resembles coarse meal. Combine the ice water, oil, egg yolk and vinegar in a mixing bowl and whisk until smooth. Add to the food processor and pulse to form a dough, adding additional ice water if needed to bind. Shape into a ball and flatten into a disk. Wrap in plastic wrap and chill in the refrigerator for 1 hour or longer.

Roll the dough into a 13-inch circle on a floured surface. Fit into the bottom and three-fourths up the side of a 9-inch springform pan; seal any cracks.

Torte: Preheat the oven to 375 degrees. Cook the sweet potatoes in a saucepan of boiling water until tender. Peel and mash the sweet potatoes; measure 3 cups, reserving any extra for another use. Combine the mashed sweet potatoes with the sweetened condensed milk, butter, eggs, honey, maple syrup, vanilla and salt in a mixing bowl. Beat until smooth.

Spoon into the prepared crust. Bake for 1 1/2 hours or until the edge begins to brown and the center is set. Cool on a wire rack for 45 minutes before serving.

Serves 16

Chef William's Prize-Winning Peach Berry Cobbler with Jalapeños

1 cup (2 sticks) butter, softened
2 1/2 cups sliced fresh or drained canned peaches
1 cup mixed berries
2 jalapeño chiles, seeded and finely minced
1 cup all-purpose flour
1 cup sugar
1 (3-ounce) package French vanilla pudding mix
1 cup milk
1 cup (2 sticks) butter, softened
1 (8-ounce) package Jiffy® corn bread mix

Preheat the oven to 350 degrees. Melt 1 cup butter in a 9×13-inch baking pan in the oven. Remove from the oven. Add the peaches, berries and jalapeño chiles to the baking pan. Mix the flour, sugar and pudding mix in a bowl. Add the milk gradually, mixing until smooth. Spoon over the fruit mixture.

Dot 1 cup butter over the corn bread mix in a bowl; mix lightly. Sprinkle over the cobbler. Bake for 1 hour. *Serves 15*

William Webster

Oatmeal Chocolate Chunk Cookies with Walnuts

1 1/4 cups rolled oats
1 cup all-purpose flour
1/2 teaspoon baking powder
1/2 teaspoon baking soda
1/2 teaspoon salt
1/2 cup (1 stick) butter, softened
1/2 cup granulated sugar
1/2 cup packed brown sugar
1 egg
1/2 teaspoon vanilla extract
3/4 cup semisweet chocolate chips
1/4 cup chopped milk chocolate
1/4 cup walnuts or other nuts

Preheat the oven to 350 degrees. Mix the oats, flour, baking powder, baking soda and salt together. Cream the butter, granulated sugar and brown sugar in a mixing bowl until light and fluffy. Beat in the egg and vanilla. Add the dry ingredients and mix well. Stir in the chocolate chips, chopped chocolate and walnuts.

Shape into a log 2 inches in diameter. Cut the log into slices that measure about 3 tablespoons each. Arrange cut side down on a baking sheet. Bake for 12 to 15 minutes or until golden brown. Cool on the baking sheet for several minutes and remove to a wire rack to cool completely. *Serves 12*

Donors and Contributors

ACE Bakery Limited
American Culinary Federation
Ararat Rock Products Company
Bank of America
Mr. & Mrs James Beiswenger
Dr. & Mrs. Steve Bissette
Brad's Golf Cars, Inc.
Mrs. Edwin Brenegar
Mr. & Mrs. Abe Brenner
Mr. & Mrs. Michael Brenner
Mr. Henry Brown
Mr. & Mrs. Joe Buchanan
Mr. & Mrs. John Burress
Call-A-Nurse, LLC
Cannon Foundation
Carolina Logistics Services
Cemala Foundation, Inc.
Centenary United Methodist Church
Mr. & Mrs. Charles Chambers
Champion Industries, Inc.
Community Foundation of Greater Greensboro
Marion Stedman Covington Foundation
Ms. Sally Daniel
Mr. & Mrs. Garry Danner
DataMax Foundation
The Tom Davis Fund
Dell Corporation
Dell Foundation
Dr. & Mrs. G. Stephen Felts
Food Lion Charitable Foundation, Inc.
Forsyth County Restaurant Association
Forsyth Electrical Co.
Mr. & Mrs. T. Vernon Foster
Mr. & Mrs. John Gates
Mr. & Mrs. J. Goins
Gwyn Electrical, Plumbing, Heating & Cooling Co.
Hanesbrands, Inc.
John W. and Anna H. Hanes Foundation
Harris Teeter, Inc.
Mr. & Mrs. James Helvey
High Point Community Foundation
High Point Historical Society
Hillsdale Fund, Inc.
Home Moravian Church
Johnson Controls, Inc.
K & W Cafeterias, Inc.
Mr. Randall Kaplan and Ms. Kathy Manning
Krispy Kreme
Larson Foundation
Leadership North Carolina
Ms. Elizabeth Lewis
Lone Star Steak House & Saloon
Masco Corporation Foundation
Mr. & Mrs. Robert Mayville
Mr. & Mrs. T. Ray McKinney
New Atlantic Contracting, Inc.
Novant Health
Piedmont Ear Nose & Throat
Piedmont Federal Savings and Loan Association
Mr. Jeffrey Powell
Reynolds American
Kate B. Reynolds Charitable Trust
Richard J. & Marie M. Reynolds Foundation
Z. Smith Reynolds Foundation
Mr. & Mrs. Thomas Ross
Rotary Club of Winston-Salem
St. Paul's Episcopal Church
Samaritan Ministries
Ms. Susan Sams
Mr. & Mrs. Leo Sasaki
Shugart Family Foundation
Sodexo Foundation
Ms. Linda Spinnett
Stateside Data, Inc.
Mr. & Mrs. W. Fletcher Steele
Sterling Events Co., Inc.
Ms. Allene Stevens
SunTrust Bank
Mr. & Mrs. Dean Swindle
Dr. & Mrs. Charles Taft
Tannenbaum-Sternberger Foundation
Mr. & Mrs. William Tessien
Ms. Mary Tucker
T.W. Garner Food Company
United Guaranty Corporation
United Way of Forsyth County
Wachovia
Walmart #2472
Weaver Foundation, Inc.
Mr. & Mrs. Gilbert Whisnant
Winston-Salem Foundation
Winston-Salem State University
Dr. & Mrs. James Yopp

Index

Accompaniments. *See also* Glazes; Sauces
    Chipotle Mayonnaise, 61
    Far East Chopped Relish, 51
    Mango Guava Salsa, 52
    Mango Salsa, 109
    North Carolina Fresh Pico de Gallo, 51
    Pesto, 107
    Sage Browned Butter, 108

Appetizers. *See also* Dips/Spreads; Snacks
    Balsamic-Glazed Peaches with Prosciutto, 35
    Cheese Grits Cakes, 30
    Chicken and Sun-Dried Tomato Meatballs, 33
    Chicken Satay, 33
    Corn and Leek Pancakes, 29
    Crab Cakes, 29
    Fried Green Tomatoes with Boursin, Bacon and Chives, 37
    Grilled Asparagus with Prosciutto, 32
    Meatballs in Chipotle Sauce, 34
    Pulled Pork Crostini, 36
    Seared Ahi Tuna on Won Ton Crisps with Wasabi Whipped Cream and Soy Reduction, 39
    Seared Grits Cakes with Crisp Country Ham and Chiffonade of Collards, 31
    Spanakopita, 27
    Teriyaki Pineapple with Brie, Bacon and Chiles, 35
    Tomato and Fresh Mozzarella Napoleons with Flash-Fried Prawns, 38

Apple
    Classic Tarte Tatin, 133
    Whipped Sweet Potatoes with Roasted Granny Smith Apples, 116

Asparagus
    Asparagus and Spinach Salad with Raspberry Vinaigrette, 42
    Crispy Grilled Duck Breasts with Pan-Caramelized Local Peaches, White Asparagus and Port Reduction, 87
    Grilled Asparagus with Prosciutto, 32

Bacon
    Barbecued Baked Beans, 81
    Fried Green Tomatoes with Boursin, Bacon and Chives, 37
    Loaded Baked Potato Salad, 47
    Teriyaki Pineapple with Brie, Bacon and Chiles, 35

Basic Brine for Poultry or Pork, 62

Beans
    Barbecued Baked Beans, 81
    Bayou Bean Soup, 13
    Black Bean and Ham Chili, 22
    Chili Con Carne TCK, 23
    Down Home Chili Beans with Beef, 72
    Minestrone, 19
    Navy Bean and Ham Soup, 13
    Pasta e Fagioli, 14
    Red Beans and Rice, 74
    White Chicken Chili, 21

Beef
    Braised Beef Ribs, 69
    Chili Con Carne TCK, 23
    Down Home Chili Beans with Beef, 72
    Meatballs in Chipotle Sauce, 34
    Meat Sauce, 73
    Santa Maria-Style Barbecued Tri-Tip Beef Roast, 71
    Teriyaki-Seared Sirloin, 96
    Texas Barbecued Beef Brisket, 70
    Veal Marsala, 96

Berries
    Asparagus and Spinach Salad with Raspberry Vinaigrette, 42
    Chef William's Prize-Winning Peach Berry Cobbler with Jalapeños, 136
    Fresh Mozzarella and Summer Strawberry Salad with Honey Balsamic Dressing, 43
    Orange Cranberry Cake, 124
    Orange Cranberry Glaze, 124

Breads
    Buttermilk Biscuits, 84
    Butterscotch Biscuits, 84
    Cheese Biscuits, 84
    Cinnamon Raisin Biscuits, 84
    Mexican Corn Bread, 83
    Orange Biscuits, 84
    Raisin Biscuits, 84
    Scotch Scones, 84
    Sugared Biscuits, 84
    Whole Wheat Biscuits, 84

Broccoli
    Cream of Broccoli Soup, 15
    Pasta Primavera, 79
    Pasta Vegetable Medley, 80
    Savory Rotini Salad, 49

Cakes
    Cinnamon Wine Cake, 120

Kentucky Butter Rum Cake, 121
Orange Cranberry Cake, 124
Pink Lemonade Cake, 123
Rum Carrot Cake, 122
Seven-Flavor Pound Cake, 119
Sweet Potato Cake, 125

Carrots
Ballymoe (Irish Stew), 24
Carrot Cheesecake, 129
Chicken Tortilla Soup, 16
Island Vegetable Medley, 115
Pasta Primavera, 79
Rum Carrot Cake, 122
Sautéed Chicken with Garden Herb Cream Sauce and Julienned Vegetables, 89
Savory Rotini Salad, 49
Vanilla-Scented Baby Vegetables, 114

Cheese
Baked Halibut with Spinach, Feta and Pignoli, 104
Cara Cara Orange Salad with Fennel Vinaigrette, Pine Nuts, Ricotta Salata and Mint, 44
Cheese Biscuits, 84
Cheese Grits Cakes, 30
Chicken Parmigiano, 93
Chive Parmesan Crackers, 32
Four-Cheese Chicken Lasagna, 77
Fresh Mozzarella and Summer Strawberry Salad with Honey Balsamic Dressing, 43
Fried Green Tomatoes with Boursin, Bacon and Chives, 37
Italian Cheese Chicken, 76
Smokin' Pimento Cheese Spread, 28
Teriyaki Pineapple with Brie, Bacon and Chiles, 35
Tomato and Fresh Mozzarella Napoleons with Flash-Fried Prawns, 38

Cheesecakes
Basic Cheesecake, 127
Carrot Cheesecake, 129
Peppermint Cheesecake, 128
Tiramisu Cheesecake, 130

Chicken
Chicken and Dumplings, 75
Chicken and Sun-Dried Tomato Meatballs, 33
Chicken Corn Chowder, 17
Chicken Noodle Soup TCK, 16
Chicken Parmigiano, 93
Chicken Satay, 33
Chicken Tortilla Soup, 16
Coq au Vin, 92
Creamy Sauce, 77
Four-Cheese Chicken Lasagna, 77
Garlic-Crusted Chicken Breasts with Summer Butter Sauce, 88
Grandma's Country Chicken Soup, 15
Grilled Chicken Pasta with Vodka Sauce, 94
Grilled Chicken Salad, 41
Italian Cheese Chicken, 76
Sautéed Chicken with Garden Herb Cream Sauce and Julienned Vegetables, 89
Sautéed Chicken with Peaches, Country Ham and Black Pepper Triple Sec Cream, 90
Shark Fin Chicken with Rum Basil Cream Sauce, 91
Texas Pete® Buffalo Chicken Dip, 28
White Chicken Chili, 21

Chili/Stews
Ballymoe (Irish Stew), 24
Black Bean and Ham Chili, 22
Chili Con Carne TCK, 23
Down Home Chili Beans with Beef, 72
White Chicken Chili, 21

Chocolate
Chocolate Caramel Macadamia Tart, 134
Oatmeal Chocolate Chunk Cookies with Walnuts, 137
Tiramisu Cheesecake, 130

Chowders
Chicken Corn Chowder, 17
Clam Chowder, 17
Roasted Red Pepper Seafood Chowder, 18
Sweet Corn Chowder, 18

Corn
Chicken Corn Chowder, 17
Corn and Leek Pancakes, 29
Mexican Corn Bread, 83
Sweet Corn Chowder, 18

Crab Meat
Crab Cakes, 29
Seafood Pasta Salad, 50

Desserts. *See also* Cakes; Cheesecakes; Frostings/Icings; Sauces, Sweet
Atchafalaya Bread Pudding with Caramel Rum Sauce, 131

Chef William's Prize-Winning Peach Berry
    Cobbler with Jalapeños, 136
Chocolate Caramel Macadamia Tart, 134
Classic Tarte Tatin, 133
Oatmeal Chocolate Chunk Cookies with
    Walnuts, 137
Paula's Sweet Potato Bread Pudding with
    Pecan Crumble, 132
Sweet Potato Torte, 135

Dips/Spreads
Smokin' Pimento Cheese Spread, 28
Texas Pete® Buffalo Chicken Dip, 28

Duck
Crispy Grilled Duck Breasts with Pan-
    Caramelized Local Peaches, White
    Asparagus and Port Reduction, 87
Sautéed Marinated Duck Breasts with Orange
    Brandy Demi-Glace, 95

Edible Parmesan Crisp Bowls, 66

Fish
Baked Halibut with Spinach, Feta and
    Pignoli, 104
Blackened Red Snapper with Cajun
    Hollandaise Sauce, 105
Chile-Rubbed Tuna with Mango Salsa, 109
Hazelnut-Seared Catfish with Chive Beurre
    Blanc, 103
Pecan-Crusted Mountain Trout with Sage
    Browned Butter, 108
Pesto Salmon, 107
Roasted Red Pepper Seafood Chowder, 18
Seared Ahi Tuna on Won Ton Crisps with
    Wasabi Whipped Cream and Soy
    Reduction, 39

Frostings/Icings
Maple Cream Cheese Frosting, 126
Rum Icing, 122

Fruit. *See also* Apple; Berries; Orange; Peach;
    Pineapple; Salads, Fruit
Apricot Ginger Couscous, 42
Mango Guava Salsa, 52
Mango Salsa, 109
Watermelon Barbecue Sauce, 55

Glazes
Balsamic Glaze, 54
Brandy Wine Glaze, 120
Lemonade Glaze, 123

Orange Cranberry Glaze, 124
Orange Sesame Glaze, 58
Seven-Flavor Glaze, 119

Greens
Chef Pam's Chipotle-Crusted Pork
    Tenderloin, 99
Chef Pam's Collard Greens, 81
Seared Grits Cakes with Crisp Country Ham
    and Chiffonade of Collards, 31

Grits
Cheese Grits Cakes, 30
Seared Grits Cakes with Crisp Country Ham
    and Chiffonade of Collards, 31

Ham
Balsamic-Glazed Peaches with
    Prosciutto, 35
Bayou Bean Soup, 13
Black Bean and Ham Chili, 22
Grilled Asparagus with Prosciutto, 32
Navy Bean and Ham Soup, 13
Pasta e Fagioli, 14
Rollatini Con Brisco, 102
Sautéed Chicken with Peaches, Country Ham
    and Black Pepper Triple Sec Cream, 90
Seared Grits Cakes with Crisp Country Ham
    and Chiffonade of Collards, 31

Lamb
Ballymoe (Irish Stew), 24
Grilled Lamb with Hazelnut Sauce, 97

Leeks
Corn and Leek Pancakes, 29
Spanakopita, 27

Lentil Soup, 19

Mushrooms
Coq au Vin, 92
Mushroom Sauce, 76
Pasta Vegetable Medley, 80
Veal Marsala, 96

Nuts
Baked Halibut with Spinach, Feta and
    Pignoli, 104
Cara Cara Orange Salad with Fennel
    Vinaigrette, Pine Nuts, Ricotta Salata and
    Mint, 44
Chocolate Caramel Macadamia Tart, 134
Grilled Lamb with Hazelnut Sauce, 97

Hazelnut-Seared Catfish with Chive Beurre Blanc, 103
Oatmeal Chocolate Chunk Cookies with Walnuts, 137
Paula's Sweet Potato Bread Pudding with Pecan Crumble, 132
Pecan-Crusted Mountain Trout with Sage Browned Butter, 108
Pecan-Crusted Pork Loin with Sweet Potato Mash and Maple Hoisin Sauce, 98
Pork Tenderloin Amandine, 100

Orange
Blood Orange Sauce, 56
Cara Cara Orange Salad with Fennel Vinaigrette, Pine Nuts, Ricotta Salata and Mint, 44
Ginger-Seared Scallops with Blood Orange Sauce, 111
Orange Biscuits, 84
Orange Brandy Demi-Glace, 95
Orange Cranberry Cake, 124
Orange Cranberry Glaze, 124
Orange Sesame Glaze, 58
Sautéed Marinated Duck Breasts with Orange Brandy Demi-Glace, 95
Savory Rotini Salad, 49

Pasta
Chicken Noodle Soup TCK, 16
Chicken Parmigiano, 93
Four-Cheese Chicken Lasagna, 77
Grilled Chicken Pasta with Vodka Sauce, 94
Mediterranean Squash Blend with Pasta, 80
Minestrone, 19
Pasta e Fagioli, 14
Pasta Primavera, 79
Pasta Vegetable Medley, 80
Pesto Salmon, 107
Rustic Tuscan Pasta with Shrimp and Sausage, 113
Sautéed Shrimp Scampi, 112

Peach
Balsamic-Glazed Peaches with Prosciutto, 35
Chef William's Prize-Winning Peach Berry Cobbler with Jalapeños, 136
Crispy Grilled Duck Breasts with Pan-Caramelized Local Peaches, White Asparagus and Port Reduction, 87
Jicama Peach Slaw, 45
Sautéed Chicken with Peaches, Country Ham and Black Pepper Triple Sec Cream, 90

Peppers
Bayou Bean Soup, 13
Chicken Tortilla Soup, 16
Greek Orzo Salad, 47
Island Vegetable Medley, 115
Mango Guava Salsa, 52
Mediterranean Squash Blend with Pasta, 80
Panzanella, 45
Roasted Red Pepper Seafood Chowder, 18
Sautéed Chicken with Garden Herb Cream Sauce and Julienned Vegetables, 89

Pineapple
Far East Chopped Relish, 51
Teriyaki Pineapple with Brie, Bacon and Chiles, 35
Wild Game Bourbon Sauce, 56

Pork. See also Bacon; Ham; Sausage
Barbecued Pork Ribs with Watermelon Barbecue Sauce, 74
Chef Pam's Chipotle-Crusted Pork Tenderloin, 99
Meatballs in Chipotle Sauce, 34
Pecan-Crusted Pork Loin with Sweet Potato Mash and Maple Hoisin Sauce, 98
Pork Tenderloin Amandine, 100
Pulled Pork Crostini, 36
Rollatini Con Brisco, 102
Southwestern Pork Medallions, 101

Potatoes
Ballymoe (Irish Stew), 24
Chef Pam's Potato Salad, 46
Chicken Corn Chowder, 17
Clam Chowder, 17
Loaded Baked Potato Salad, 47
Roasted Red Pepper Seafood Chowder, 18
Sweet Corn Chowder, 18

Rice
Coconut Rice, 82
Red Beans and Rice, 74

Rubs/Seasonings
Cajun Seasoning, 65
Chef Jeff's Barbecue Rub, 64
Chipotle Dry Rub, 63
Dry Rub, 41
Sachet D'Epices, 65
Seasoning Salt, 71

Salad Dressings
Citrus Sherry Vinaigrette, 60

Fennel Vinaigrette, 44
Honey Balsamic Dressing, 60
Raspberry Vinaigrette, 42
Red Wine Vinaigrette, 61
Wine Vinaigrette, 49
Zesty Dressing, 50

Salads
Apricot Ginger Couscous, 42
Asparagus and Spinach Salad with Raspberry Vinaigrette, 42
Fresh Mozzarella and Summer Strawberry Salad with Honey Balsamic Dressing, 43
Grilled Chicken Salad, 41
Panzanella, 45

Salads, Fruit
Cara Cara Orange Salad with Fennel Vinaigrette, Pine Nuts, Ricotta Salata and Mint, 44
Jicama Peach Slaw, 45

Salads, Pasta
Greek Orzo Salad, 47
Savory Rotini Salad, 49
Seafood Pasta Salad, 50

Salads, Vegetable
Chef Pam's Potato Salad, 46
Loaded Baked Potato Salad, 47

Sauces, Savory
Alfredo Sauce, 54
Blood Orange Sauce, 56
Cajun Hollandaise Sauce, 57
Chipotle Sauce, 34
Chive Beurre Blanc, 103
Classic Velouté, 59
Creamy Sauce, 77
Demi-Glace, 59
Espagnole Sauce, 58
Hazelnut Sauce, 97
Meat Sauce, 73
Mushroom Sauce, 76
Orange Brandy Demi-Glace, 95
Rum Basil Cream Sauce, 91
Watermelon Barbecue Sauce, 55
Wild Game Bourbon Sauce, 56

Sauces, Sweet
Butter Rum Sauce, 121
Caramel Rum Sauce, 131
Lemonade Sauce, 123

Sausage
Red Beans and Rice, 74
Rustic Tuscan Pasta with Shrimp and Sausage, 113

Seafood. *See also* Crab Meat; Fish; Shrimp
Butter-Poached Lobster, 110
Clam Chowder, 17
Ginger-Seared Scallops with Blood Orange Sauce, 111

Shrimp
Rustic Tuscan Pasta with Shrimp and Sausage, 113
Sautéed Shrimp Scampi, 112
Seafood Pasta Salad, 50
Tomato and Fresh Mozzarella Napoleons with Flash-Fried Prawns, 38

Snacks
Chive Parmesan Crackers, 32
Parmesan Crisps, 66

Soups. *See also* Chili/Stews; Chowders
Bayou Bean Soup, 13
Chicken Noodle Soup TCK, 16
Chicken Tortilla Soup, 16
Chilled Gazpacho, 20
Cream of Broccoli Soup, 15
Creamy Tomato Basil Soup, 21
Grandma's Country Chicken Soup, 15
Lentil Soup, 19
Minestrone, 19
Navy Bean and Ham Soup, 13
Pasta e Fagioli, 14
Tomato Bisque, 20

Spinach
Asparagus and Spinach Salad with Raspberry Vinaigrette, 42
Baked Halibut with Spinach, Feta and Pignoli, 104
Pesto Salmon, 107
Spanakopita, 27

Squash
Island Vegetable Medley, 115
Mediterranean Squash Blend with Pasta, 80
Pasta Primavera, 79
Vanilla-Scented Baby Vegetables, 114

Stocks
Basic Chicken Stock, 63
Brown Beef Stock, 62

Sweet Potatoes
  Paula's Sweet Potato Bread Pudding with
    Pecan Crumble, 132
  Sweet Potato Cake, 125
  Sweet Potato Casserole, 82
  Sweet Potato Mash, 98
  Sweet Potato Torte, 135
  Whipped Sweet Potatoes with Roasted Granny
    Smith Apples, 116

Tomatoes
  Chicken and Sun-Dried Tomato Meatballs, 33
  Creamy Tomato Basil Soup, 21
  Fried Green Tomatoes with Boursin, Bacon
    and Chives, 37
  Greek Orzo Salad, 47
  North Carolina Fresh Pico de Gallo, 51

Panzanella, 45
Tomato and Fresh Mozzarella Napoleons with
  Flash-Fried Prawns, 38
Tomato Bisque, 20

Turkey Potpie Casserole, 78

Vegetables. *See also* Asparagus; Beans; Broccoli;
  Carrots; Corn; Greens; Leeks; Mushrooms;
  Peppers; Potatoes; Salads, Vegetable;
  Spinach; Squash; Sweet Potatoes; Tomatoes
Chilled Gazpacho, 20
Far East Chopped Relish, 51
Island Vegetable Medley, 115
Mediterranean Squash Blend with Pasta, 80
Minestrone, 19
Vanilla-Scented Baby Vegetables, 114

To order additional copies of

TESTED BY
fire
TRIAD
COMMUNITY
KITCHEN

contact

Second Harvest Food Bank of Northwest North Carolina
3655 Reed Street
Winston-Salem, North Carolina 27107
Telephone: (336) 784-5770
Fax: (336) 784-7369
Web site: www.hungernwnc.org